RENEWED
POWER
FOR
PREACHING

RENEWED POWER FOR PREACHING

Glenn H. Asquith

Judson Press® Valley Forge

RENEWED POWER FOR PREACHING

Library of Congress Cataloging in Publication Data

Asquith, Glenn H.
  Renewed power for preaching.

  1. Preaching   I. Title.
BV4211.2.A82   1983   251   83-11327
ISBN 0-8170-1003-3

The name JUDSON PRESS is registered as a trademark in the U.S. Patent Office.
Printed in the U.S.A. ✠

Dedicated with love
to my son
Glenn H. Asquith, Jr., Ph.D.,
teacher of preachers

"It is stern work, it is perilous work, to thrust your
hand in the sun
And pull out a spark of immortal flame to warm the
hearts of men. . . ."*

*"The Proud Poet" by Joyce Kilmer from *Main Street and Other Poems*. (New York: George H. Doran Co., 1917), p. 37. Copyright 1916 by Kenton Kilmer. Reprinted by permission of Doubleday & Company, Inc.

Preface

Tunnelers cutting a road through a hill use various tools: earth-moving machines, picks, crowbars, shovels, pneumatic drills, and hammers. But when they come to a solid rock face, they find that these implements are insufficient. Then they call in the dynamite people. The dynamite people are the *dunamis*—the power people. The power people put charges in the rock and blast away the obstruction that blocks the way of the other workmen, keeping them from going on into the light on the other side of the towering elevation.

As we view our world today, we are agonizingly aware that a great mass of seemingly impenetrable breadth and unscalable height confronts us all. In this mass we can distinguish outcroppings of despair, hate, prejudice, violence, greed, ignorance, suffering, lust for power, materialism, perversion, faithlessness, godlessness, uncontrolled appetites, selfishness, and, over all, the haze of hopelessness. At the heart of this mountain is the geological force of sin that has been producing the whole mass through long generations. Indeed, as the Brazilians of Rio de Janeiro call their geological eminence "Sugarloaf Mountain," we may call our spiritual one "Sinloaf Mountain."

And how do we propose to make our way through this mass that circumscribes our journey toward goodness and God? Certain tools are brought to the scene to do some chipping. We place confidence in the parleys of the United Nations, the work of psychiatry and psychology, educational systems, social welfare programs, and disarmament discussions. We trust in gurus, many varieties of meditation, the return of Atlantis, parapsychology, occult cults, self-realization groups, astrology, and splinter churches of strange names and aims. But, eventually, all of these—some worthy—come to the solid rock face. Now, where are the power people to come to the rescue? Where is the spiritual and social dynamite that can match this need?

We know that that sorely needed power resides only in God. And who can best apply that power to our present necessity? Who can instruct in the use of that power so that the solid rock face in human hearts and in social institutions and governments shall yield and crumble until the light shines upon us? Who best but the preachers anointed to proclaim the Good News?

Contents

Introduction

If a person has something of value to deliver to another person, there are three factors involved—the preparation and skill of the deliverer, the worth of the item being delivered, and the vehicle that will carry the item.

To follow the analogy, the preacher is the delivering person, the item to be delivered is the Word of God, and the vehicle is the sermon. By examination it would seem that the vehicle is the least important of the three factors in each case.

However, the vehicle of the preacher—the sermon—seems to be given top priority in classes in homiletics. What the message of God is and what sort of person the preacher must be are given less attention.

With this situation in mind the author has thought it worthwhile to collect into one book the results and accretions of years of experience, study, consultation, prayer, and meditation involved in the agonizing struggle to be a preacher.

At the beginning it is necessary for the preacher to have a full and reverent estimation of what he or she has chosen, from among all other possible pursuits, to do for a lifetime. To be a preacher is an overwhelming and mysterious thing. This description of preaching may give some idea of this:

Preaching is like nothing else in all the wide world. And no other than a preacher can know the feeling of compassion and utter inadequaçy as he stands before a congregation awaiting a word from God. There are the people—men, women, young people, boys, and girls—with problems too deep for tears, temptations too strong to resist alone, with guilt, longing, anxiety, uncertainty, pain. And there is the preacher to whom they all look for the word that will send them back into the world with confidence, courage, and a sense of warm forgiveness.[1]

These chapters will take the stance of being in awe before the office of the preacher. The preacher will be shown as one who has been to Sinai and on the road to Damascus.

1

The Preacher's Credentials

"Why am *I* a preacher?"

"Is preaching, after all, the task for which I am best equipped?"

"Has my preaching made anything of importance happen?"

These three questions come to every preacher sooner or later. In fact, they surface many times as the years go on. Answers must be found if the preacher is to go on with the work in an effective, confident way, affirming that God is an ever-present partner in all that is done.

Happily, there is an answer to each of the questions, an answer that may be found by reexamining the preacher's credentials. These credentials may be gathered up under three headings: call, gift, and power.

In this chapter we will look at the general substance of the major credentials; the remaining chapters will bring out the results accruing to the preacher when these are markedly possessed.

We start with the call, the answer to "Why am *I* a preacher?" According to the judgment of our forefathers, the call was the prime qualification for a preacher. Even today the call is recognized, although in a less arbitrary manner. Indeed, included in one set of questions put to a candidate for ordination is a question on this order: "Do you *think* you are called?" The required answer is "I think so." To carry a preacher through the long years of service, the assurance of the call needs to be much deeper than *thinking*.

An illustration of the experience of the called and uncalled may be found in the account of Ahimaaz in the Old Testament. King David's son Absalom had been killed in battle, and Joab, the military commander, chose a Cushite to run with the news to David. But Ahimaaz said, "Let me also run after the Cushite." Joab tried to discourage him, but he insisted, "I will run." So Ahimaaz ran and arrived before the presence of the king before the slower Cushite. But when the king inquired for the news, Ahimaaz lost his nerve and said, "I saw a great tumult, but I do not know what it was" (2 Samuel 18:19-30). This same thing can happen to uncalled people who, on their own initiative, decide to preach. They select the task for themselves, but when the crucial moment for telling the Good News is upon them, they falter. We must, and can, believe that God singles out, and has always singled out, the ones who are to bear the tidings as preachers.

There are others who do not presume to become preachers but are practically thrust into the ministry by well-meaning parents or friends. The end result is what history shows us to have been the case in the Church of England when younger sons of families were assigned by their fathers to the church. The elder sons inherited titles and estates or went into the military; so what was left for a well-bred young man but the church? This accounted for much of the languid condition of the church that brought forth the renewal under John Wesley—a truly called man. Many churches in our day are in sore straits and look for preaching that will reflect the experience of the call.

Another unhappy result of being without the call is that "professionalism" takes hold and would-be preachers become overly selective about the social and financial advantages to be had in the opportunities available to them.

Thinking of these unhappy results of the lack of direction, we may well ask how it is possible to know that the call has come. A quick survey of how it was with the prophets and apostles as recorded in the Bible is enough to point the way. Two statements, in particular, of divinely called preachers may serve as good guides: Isaiah stated his credential of the call when he said:

> The Spirit of the Lord God is upon me,
> because the LORD has anointed me
> to bring good tidings . . . .
> —Isaiah 61:1

And Paul, about whom no doubt can be raised concerning the call, said, "Woe to me if I do not preach the gospel! For if I do this of my own will, I have a reward; but if not of my own will, I am entrusted with a commission" (1 Corinthians 9:16b-17).

These Scripture verses illustrate the obligatory nature of preaching. The preacher is doing what cannot be avoided except at the price of inner agony. True preaching is not done by human choice, and all worldly rewards cannot equal the inner sense of having fulfilled the Lord's commission.

Thus, the question "Why am *I* a preacher?" is answered, "Because God has *called me* to preach."

The answer to the second question, "Is preaching, after all, the task for which I am best equipped?" will be found in the credential of the gift. Could we think that God would call anyone without providing the necessary qualifications?

Primarily, the gift is that of the Spirit. We know that Peter received a commission from Jesus: "Feed my lambs. . . . Tend my sheep. . . . Feed my sheep" (John 21:15-17). But we know, too, that Peter did not have the essential gift that prepared him for preaching until the Spirit was given to him at Pentecost. With this gift, Peter preached a sermon that resulted in the conversion of three thousand souls (Acts 2:41). How, we may inquire, was Peter after Pentecost different from Peter before Pentecost? Undoubtedly, he was the same fisherman. His traits of being bluff, aggressive, and impetuous were not altered. His store of general knowledge had not increased. He had no more formal education than before. How, then, did the gift of the Spirit use this same man in a situation that called for so much courage, forthrightness, and skill in the selection of words? This process, of course, cannot be explained fully in human terms. Some light must be found.

At the outset we may remind ourselves that "we have this treasure in earthen vessels" (2 Corinthians 4:7). Even if Peter had been a doctor of laws—a man reared to the highest standards of learning and culture, with the ability to speak logically and persuasively, and with a noble family background—he would still have been an earthen vessel in contrast to the preciousness of the gospel, which he was called to proclaim. With this in mind, our common method of assessing present-day preachers by answering the question "Is he the one most likely to succeed?" will need to be reconsidered. The degree of difference may be as small as that between an antique article and one made yesterday. The antique may be two thousand years old, but the difference between one day and two thousand years is as nothing when contrasted to the age of the world or to eternity. With preachers the differential is the gift of the Spirit. Peter without the Spirit would have been just another fisherman; Paul without the Spirit would have continued as an inveterate persecutor of others.

This is not to say that all talents, inherited good traits, and acquired excellencies are not of value in preaching. The point is that none of these desirable qualities is a prerequisite in God's sight. Later we shall explore how God expects the best from his preachers, but for now, perhaps, we may join in refusing to endorse the position of an early group of Swedish Baptists who were suspicious of an "educated ministry." While we may heartily agree with their premise that education is no substitute for the unction of the Spirit, we do not discount the added value of preparation.

The gift of the Spirit acts to open the floodgates of a preacher's being. All that the person possesses may be backed up behind a dam that permits no more than a mere trickle of one's total ability and fervor to flow forth. But when the gates are opened to the fullest, every iota of experience, knowledge, understanding, and desire to communicate gush out without impediment. Diffidence, fear, and self-distrust are swept aside in the rush of total mobilization.

As everything is brought into action in one grand maneuver, each preaching experience may become a Waterloo that will not allow anything to be held in reserve. At the historical Waterloo the victory went to the forces under Wellington because of the total involvement of his forces. Napoleon, with all of his military genius, had forces that were to come into battle in due time. However, those forces were delayed and misguided and arrived after the battle had been decided. For a preacher, only the gift of the Spirit makes possible the utilization of all that the preacher has to bring to bear. Thus, a person with minimal abilities, according to the world's standards, may preach with greater force and result than a more highly endowed individual who uses only part of what is within. Thus it was with Peter the fisherman. The Spirit channeled all of his "littles" and made something great of the combination. The thoughts of a poet (quoted by Winston Churchill in wartime) express something of this.

> For while the tired waves, vainly breaking,
> Seem here no painful inch to gain,
> Far back, through creeks and inlets making,
> Comes silent, flooding, in the main . . . .[1]

From the many small creeks and inlets of the preacher's being, the Spirit draws all into the mainstream of one great endeavor.

Thus, the question "Is preaching, after all, the task for which I am best equipped?" is answered by the credential of the gift. "Yes, this task is what I am best equipped to do because I have the gift of the Spirit."

Going on to the third question, "Has my preaching made anything of importance happen?" we look to the third credential—power.

When a huge utility company sends out its annual report to stockholders, a map is usually included on which is marked the locations of its power plants. Each of these installations generates power to supply light, heat, and energy to the surrounding area. Surely, when God calls a person to be a preacher, that person is pinpointed as one of God's power sources in the world; the people in the area around that preacher will have God's power available to them. The preacher stands in the position of one who has been chosen to be a conductor of God's light, loving warmth, and unexcelled energy to humankind. We might well consider it a great and triumphant victory for the gospel if every preacher in the world faithfully exercised this transference of power.

The fact that spiritual power is not being radiated from all preaching points was suspected by theologian Reinhold Niebuhr and scientist Charles Steinmetz. Neibuhr is quoted as having said: "The kingdoms of the world fear only power. Religion is, after all, a very innocuous vagary."[2] And Steinmetz (called a wizard in harnessing electrical power) stated: "The greatest power of all is in our midst unscratched today. I refer to the spiritual power that comes through right living and worship."[3] Among the ingredients of readiness of a preacher, power must be considered one of the essentials.

Electric power discloses itself by happenings. If we have doubts that there is power in the cable connecting the house with the main line on the pole outside, we may test this by flicking on the light, the TV, or some appliance. If something happens, there is power; if nothing happens, power is absent. If the owner of a car doubts that there is gasoline in the tank and power in the battery under the hood, a turn of the ignition key will disclose the availability or unavailability of propelling power. Similar trials of preaching may be made. Does anything happen during or after preaching? Is the status quo of the hearers, the society, or the larger world affected at all? Wherever Paul went, there was never any doubt that he was a carrier of power. Things happened and his adversaries complained, "These men who have turned the world upside down have come here also" (Acts 17:6).

When the disciples went about the countryside preaching after Pentecost, things happened that are mentioned often in the New Testament. One expression that recurs frequently in the Greek of the book of Acts (e.g., Acts 5:12) is *sameia kai terata* (signs and wonders). Power was undeniably demonstrated.

Fortunately for the world, the appearance of preachers with power did not end with the early church. The history of preaching shows a rich galaxy of such persons, among whom were Martin Luther in Germany, John Calvin in Switzerland, John Wesley and William Booth in England, and George Whitefield and Dwight L. Moody in America. These preachers shared the destiny of peoples and nations. Those who have taken up the same torch are to be found in abundance today.

The question arises, however, as to what kinds of "signs and wonders" and world shaking events are to be expected of us in our time? The New Testament physical healings, demon displacement, and restorations to life are rarely represented in our contemporary preaching. What then? Before exploring this further, we should pause long enough to admit our inner feelings of inadequacy in not having sufficient faith for this variety of "signs and wonders" and to look longingly at the mountains we have not been able to remove. Also, it is important to cling to the sure knowledge that "with God all things are possible" (Matthew 19:26).

It may be, too, that present-day preachers are doing more of this kind of power working than is readily seen. To illustrate: there is what is called "time-lapse photography," in which a motion picture may be speeded up to portray a process that has taken days or months. A flower may be shown coming into bloom before our eyes in a moment of time, whereas we might sit in our garden for several days before we could see this entire happening. A gradual eclipse of the sun may be replayed for us on TV in a matter of minutes. Perhaps if we could see the final result of our preaching in the healing of persons, their return to newness of life, and the dispelling of ingrown habits and prejudices and vices, we might be amazed at the great things that are being done through the power of God. Must we not believe the promise ". . . he who believes in me will also do the works that I do; and greater works than these will he do . . ." (John 14:12)?

Does not a church to which a preacher comes as spiritual leader have a right to expect that that person will have some power to nurture the church, to bring joy and peace among the gathered people, and to move all toward a mission of evangelism and reconciliation? And does not the community in which the church is located have the right to expect that the presence of the preacher will be a benediction and a challenge to better living? (It was said of Phillips Brooks that he needed only to walk along the streets of the city to bring joy and a sense of God's love.) Does not the church at large have the right to expect of any preacher that his or her God-given power will add to the spiritual victories of the larger fellowship?

So we find that the third question, "Has my preaching made anything of importance happen?" is answered: "My preaching has made more things of supreme importance happen than I can possibly estimate or know, because I have been God's conductor of power."

If, then, a preacher finds the three troublesome questions answered, is there anything else to be considered? Yes, there is one other pertinent matter with which to deal. This may be illustrated by the image of a fine violinist. A well-prepared and talented musician may have an instrument made by a master craftsman on which he is to play the compositions that will move people to the heights of joy and inspiration. Does this violinist merely pick up the violin casually and stand before the audience and perform? It is not that easy. The musician keeps the instrument in excellent condition. The strings are replaced when worn; the bow is waxed. And, above all else, the musician tunes the violin carefully before daring to play for expectant people. There is a lesson for all preachers here.

In the glow and awe of receiving a call to preach, one may experience the temptation to say with the emperor Sigismund, *"Ego sum rex Romanus, et supra grammaticam."* ("I am the Roman king, and above grammar.") The fact is, however, that the call, the gift, and the power do not obviate keeping the preaching instrument tuned and in the best of condition. Continued training for the mighty task should be a lifetime endeavor of the preacher.

Jesus, himself, showed us the way in this. We find that the Lord as a lad talked to the learned teachers of the law in the temple. He stayed in the home of Joseph and Mary for many years, subject to their guidance. He came to John the Baptist. He was forty days in the wilderness, gaining strength for the coming privation, experiencing the force of temptation, and envisioning his mission. At other times he went apart to commune with God (as in Gethsemane). And the result was that ". . .he knew all men and needed no one to bear witness of man; for he himself knew what was in man" (John 2:25). We remember, too, that the twelve men whom Jesus called to follow him were not sent out to preach until after they had been prepared by him.

Year after year the preacher will need to read widely to keep abreast of theological and secular thought and discoveries. He or she should also be eager to take advantage of opportunities for continuing education, going through the world as a seeker of truth. The preacher should never be fearful of letting the events and the thinking of the world pass through the sieve of the faith he or she holds. Perhaps a careful pondering of this statement by a mid-nineteenth-century British preacher may serve as a rebuke if we ever grow weary of our search for improvement.

> It is true that, to the wise of this world, the cross in itself is "foolishness;" but Christ never sent fools to be its heralds. The institution of preaching, as the means for regenerating mankind, is in itself "foolishness;" but none of the preachers sent of God were simpletons.[4]

The chapters that follow are designed to open up some vistas of thought as we explore the richness hidden in the three major credentials of preaching.

2

Preaching from the Minister's Cross

"All who have meant good work with their whole hearts, have done good work, although they may die before they have the time to sign it."[1] This statement of Robert Louis Stevenson is a good incentive to get on with whatever task is at hand, and it is applicable to most endeavors. But there is an exception. Preaching is the exception. Preaching must always be signed, and the signature on preaching is the cross.

Jesus preached: ". . . he who does not take his cross and follow me is not worthy of me" (Matthew 10:38). He signed this preaching by carrying *his* cross to Golgotha and by dying upon it. Jesus preached: "Greater love has no man than this, that a man lay down his life for his friends. You are my friends . . ." (John 15:13-14). He signed this sermon by displaying his love on the cross. Indeed, an analysis of the total content of Jesus' preaching will disclose the elements of self-denial and death.

What was true of the preaching of Jesus is true of all preaching. Just as the cross of Jesus was his signature, so must the preacher's cross sign what he or she has said. In a real sense, a preacher cannot expect to use Christ's cross as the only needed signature; the cross borne by the preacher is absolutely necessary for the world to see.

How vapid would have been Paul's preaching had it not been

signed by the dangers, trials, sufferings, hunger, and thirst that he experienced (recounted in 2 Corinthians 11:23-33)!

And the preaching of Father Damien, who originally spoke as a man with clean and wholesome flesh, was signed when he himself contracted leprosy.

But what of this signature of our cross? Most of us preachers live in a society that does not make physical martyrs of us. Due to the organization of denominations and churches, there is little difficulty in securing what the Church of England once called a "living"— that is, a parish (preaching place) paying a salary sufficient to keep us in comfort and providing a privileged place in the community, oftentimes with financial exemptions. How is a cross to be found in the midst of all of this softness?

What must be considered first is what we are offering to God. The example of King David comes to mind. In a time of national distress, David went to make an offering to God. He wished to buy from Araunah the Jebusite an altar place and animals for the sacrifice. Araunah graciously offered to *give* him what he needed, but King David refused the offer, saying, "No, but I will buy it of you for a price; I will not offer burnt offerings to the LORD my God which cost me nothing" (2 Samuel 24:24). *Cost* is the key word. Unless what we offer to God locks a door on some cherished desire, sets up a "no thoroughfare" sign on some sidepath, disturbs the easy flow of routine, or diminishes our store of nonessential acquisitions, there is no cost. Rather, there has been a gathering up of some surplus that has come without effort and is not engaging us closely. An offering, to be an offering, must be something of intimate value to the giver. When Abraham went out to offer his only son, Isaac, to the Lord his God, he knew what the offering cost. He was not asked to sacrifice his neighbor's son or the son of a stranger but his own dearly loved son (Genesis 22:1-14). Abraham knew he was giving part of himself. It was the same for Hannah when she gave her longed-for son, Samuel, to God (1 Samuel 1:26-28). Hannah knew what cost meant. And so it is with the one who heeds the call to preach; always the offering to God must cost dearly.

The truth is that the preacher's offering to God will be nothing less than the preacher's self. This gift of self will be the cross from which the preaching is done—the cross that will sign the preaching. We may understand more fully what is required by looking at the various facets of the self that will be given to God.

First, perhaps, is the giving to God of all ambition to be thought of as someone great—the desire to achieve "professional" success or preferment, to be praised by the people, to rise to positions of power and prominence in the church. In Roman Catholic circles we hear the expression "princes of the church" and in Protestant churches "princes of the pulpit." But did not Jesus say, ". . . Whoever would be great among you must be your servant, and whoever would be first among you must be your slave; even as the Son of man came not to be served but to serve . . ." (Matthew 20:26-28)? This was said in reply to the request of the mother of John and James that they be given the two choice positions in Christ's kingdom.

This is not to infer that a preacher is to be a mousy, retiring sort of person with a "back of the bus" characteristic. The preacher serves the King of kings and walks through the world without apology. And if a preacher gives unstintedly to the calling, a situation of large responsibility is likely to be offered. If the preacher is convinced that the new field of service is opened by God, well and good. But the cross ingredient is that the preacher will not begin to think of himself or herself as an unusual person, well deserving of promotion! The preacher will know that others serving in obscure spots are doing work just as worthy and essential in God's kingdom as he or she. When people begin to praise the preacher and his or her work (and, oh, how wonderful it is to hear compliments!), it is well to remember what Paul did after a healing at Lystra. The crowds shouted, "The gods have come down to us in the likeness of men!" (Acts 14:11). Paul rebuked this outcry, saying "Men, why are you doing this? We also are men, of like nature with you . . . you should turn from these vain things to a living God . . ." (Acts 14:15). Paul could, and did, point away from himself to God because he had the cross in his heart: "I have been crucified with Christ; it is no longer I who live, but Christ who lives in me . . ." (Galatians 2:20).

Marking the grandeur of the prophet's (preacher's) role in the world, George Buttrick gives this warning: "Not that his office can ever be his throne: it is his altar where life is laid down . . . It is his burden, his doom, and his exceeding joy."[2] If the preacher carries his or her cross to every preaching station and erects it over every title and distinction, the sermons will be signed.

And just as worldly ambition is placed well within the shadow of the preacher's cross, so will time and effort be in the full umbra. What Lord Cecil said of Sir Walter Raleigh, "I know that he can toil terribly,"[3] should be true of every preacher. If years of preparation and bone- and mind-breaking work is required for acceptance in the fields of medicine, law, and research sciences, how much more time and effort does the practitioner of the Word need to put into preaching! Those who train to be worthy to take care of mortal bodies, who study to be qualified to unsnarl controversies concerning material possessions, who search out the properties of the elements of the universe in order to utilize the power and potential of these elements must not be allowed to put to shame the preachers who deal with that which is eternal. Unhappily, there are times when these lay persons become suspicious that the resident preacher is not equaling their devotion and application to their jobs. The chairperson of a pulpit committee questioned a candidate on this: "How much time do you spend on your sermons? Our church has men and women in positions of responsibility. They struggle with the problems day after day, work overtime when necessary, and take work home with them. We do not want a preacher who gives us something off the top of his [or her] head."

This chairperson probably had in mind a sort of superficial, extemporaneous preaching. But can there be preaching extempore? There may be times when the preacher does not have as a background a completed manuscript resulting from many hours of study, research, meditation, thought, and prayer; but real preaching must have behind it agonized waiting for guidance and the message from the Spirit. In some fashion the requisite time and effort must be expended.

Never must a preacher be in the position of the one mentioned by Willard L. Sperry:

> No one, I think can fail to be struck by the general contrast between the precision of the work of the modern world and the vagueness of the average sermon. A friend of mine told me that on a recent occasion he heard a minister settle the problem of capital and labor in a twenty-minute sermon. He said that you had only to look at him to know that he had had no experience of capital and that after you had heard him you knew that he knew nothing about labor![4]

Also coming under the strictures of the preacher's borne cross is the firm decision to live moderately (at best), insofar as creature comforts are concerned. Although the words "abstemious" and "ascetic" have suffered a negative connotation, they are related to a cross. Both have in them two good thoughts—self-denial and discipline. Without these qualities no true cross can be borne. But this raises a question that must be answered. Where is the cutoff point between basic necessities—adequate housing, suitable and sufficient clothing, a reasonable amount of wholesome food, ample opportunities for personal enrichment (all of this for a family, too, if there is one)—and a surplus condition that amounts to an indulgent surrender to the things of the flesh? Some examples from literature may illuminate this problem.

James Michener in *Chesapeake* describes a clergyman who ate so much that he was of enormous weight—to the extent that he had to be attended by several serving men to help him rise from a chair, a boat, a carriage or other situation of recumbency. His self-indulgence extended to his insistence that he be given plots of land to make him rich. When challenged by a townsman as to what charities he was supporting, he could not name *one*. This may seem to us an exaggerated and rare type of minister, but it is disturbingly symbolic of what happens when a preacher's cross is laid down to gather dust in some obscure part of his being. A desire for getting and an emphasis on receiving soon kill a passion for giving.

At the other extreme, the poet Matthew Arnold shows us this picture:

> 'Twas August, and the fierce sun overhead
> Smote on the squalid streets of Bethnal Green,
> And the pale weaver, through his windows seen
> In Spitalfields, look'd thrice dispirited.
>
> I met a preacher there I knew, and said:
> "Ill and o'erworked, how fare you in this scene?"
> "Bravely!" said he; "for of late I have been
> Much cheer'd by thoughts of Christ, *the living bread.*"
>
> O human soul! so long as thou canst so
> Set up a mark of everlasting light. . . .
> Not with lost toil thou labourest through the night![5]

This is a symbol of the thoroughly devoted preacher, who shares the toil and deprivation of those hearing the preaching. The cross is borne truly and gladly. The sermons are signed.

The synthesis of what is possible is found in Victor Hugo's *Les Miserables.* The bishop refuses to live in the palace provided for him. From all of the good things, the perquisites permitted to his position in life, he takes only a certain amount. He accepts a small dwelling, one large enough for him, his housekeeper, and strangers who may need lodging. He accepts food that is nourishing but plain. He accepts clothing that is warm and durable without ostentation. His needs are well supplied, but luxury and surfeit are absent. He has a blessed influence in the diocese, because he directs that which he refuses for himself to fill the needs of others.

Michener's rector, Arnold's preacher, and Hugo's bishop say something to us as preachers today. We hear that our attitudes toward the creature comforts are being observed by those around us. Our deft handling of theology and our mastery of rhetoric are secondary—if noted at all—to what sort of physical discipline is discernible.

And this leads into another aspect of cross bearing. Anyone bearing a cross becomes conspicuous. The acceptance of a call to preach brings with it being singled out from among all of the uncalled. The public expects this, to our dismay. It will not do to protest that we are men and women with the same appetites, failures, and longings as other men and women. We are marked persons.

This assumption of our difference was expressed by an official in a church to which a new preacher had come. The man said to his pastor: "You will see us doing things that we never want to catch you doing!" At first the preacher thought of this statement as an indication of hypocrisy. After longer consideration, however, the pastor realized that the people in that church were hungry for an example. Just as a woman wants a pattern from which to cut a dress and a man wants angles and squares and plumb lines to enable him to build well and an artist wants a model, so people struggling in the world want a person to serve as an example of what a Christ follower can be. The specific publicity that comes when a preacher strays from the way of righteousness is prompted, perhaps, not so much by vindictiveness as by a sense of betrayal. The occupation of a person caught up in a scandal is usually of secondary news importance unless that person is a preacher! The reason may be that a teacher, for example, may break a legal or moral law without invalidating the mathematics or physics taught in the classroom, but when a preacher falters, doubt is cast on the value and power of the theology, Christian fellowship, and eternal hope that he or she has represented and offered from the pulpit.

Paul grasped this predicament as he went about preaching. Armored by his training in the law, his sophisticated background, and his ability to sift the essential seed from the nonessential chaff, he knew what he could do in his personal life that would not blunt his spiritual rectitude. But he found that there were those who were not able to make reasonable distinctions and who, from heredity or environment, feared not only the "camels" of evil but also all of the tiny "gnats." For the sake of those he sought to win for Christ, Paul decided against himself and said, "Therefore, if food is a cause of my brother's falling, I will never eat meat, lest I cause my brother to fall" (1 Corinthians 8:13). The occasion, of course, was a particular one having to do with the advisability of eating meat that had been offered in heathen temples. But the principle we get from this is that a preacher must be ready to sacrifice even innocent (to him) employments, ways of life, amusements, and desires if and when these present a stumbling block to someone in need of God. Those now being fed with the milk of the Word and not ready for the mature meat of the Word call forth from the preacher certain abstentions that must be considered carefully.

Beyond the things expected by men and women, the preacher is to pattern his or her life by the eternal verities found in the New Testament. Changing life-styles that do not conform to the basic goodness and integrity of scriptural guidance for prophets are not for the preacher. The guidelines in Timothy and Titus mark out a clear path for a cross-bearing preacher.

We have pulled out just a few of the ways the cross influences the inner and outward life of a preacher. The truth is that no area of a preacher's being is off limits to the cross, which may provoke some to say that being a preacher is an impossible, or at least undesirable, kind of existence. But did we think it would be easy? It has been reported that someone questioned Dr. Johnson, the famed English literary figure, as to whether or not the calling of a minister was an easy one. Dr. Johnson replied: "No sir, it is not easy, and I do not envy the man that makes it so."

If, then, we have established that a called preacher can only sign his sermons by preaching them from his own cross, we are ready to go on into the exciting, rejoicing, and rewarding ways that a preacher may preach. But before we close off this thought of the signing cross, it may be well to write on our minds this statement of a preacher of an earlier day, P.T. Forsyth: "If a man preach let him preach as the Oracle of God, let him preach as Christ did, whose true pulpit was His Cross. . . ."[6]

3

Conviction

A friend met David Hume, the historian and philosopher, as he was hurrying along the streets of London one day, and inquired where he was going. "To hear George Whitefield preach," was the answer. This surprised the friend for Hume was known to be unfriendly to Christianity, and he exclaimed, "Surely you do not believe what Whitefield is preaching, do you?" "No," replied Hume, "but he does."[1]

The fact that George Whitefield could and did preach from his own unshakable conviction drew even free thinkers to his congregation. There is a contagion and power in personal conviction that cannot be equaled in any other approach. Paul found this positiveness in Jesus, and he endeavored always to emulate it.

> "Do I make my plans like a worldly man, ready to say Yes and No at once? As surely as God is faithful, our word to you has not been Yes and No. For the Son of God, Jesus Christ, whom we preached among you . . . was not Yes and No; but in him it is always Yes. For all the promises of God find their Yes in him. That is why we utter the Amen through him, to the glory of God (2 Corinthians 1:17-20).

No less than in Paul's time, the preacher of today has the task of being the amen sayer to the promises of God. And let us not doubt that people are wistfully seeking certainty in their lives and that we, as preachers, have a prime opportunity for helping them find a foundation.

Perhaps at times we may be critical, contemptuous, or vaguely amused at the trend expressed in the words "I am trying to find myself." Young people leave school, get out on the roads with a backpack, go to far countries, try cults and drugs—always with the tantalizing thought that somewhere someone or something will tell them who they are and what their purpose in life is. Sometimes husbands or wives walk away from family responsibilities on the same quest. But let us remember that George Fox, who became the founder of the Society of Friends (Quakers), was one of the first to voice this need for certainty. He walked up and down the roads of England crying out, "Who will speak to my condition?" Such seekers as these, and to an extent all people are on this search, have a right to expect that we will preach from conviction.

Of course, before we can preach with strong conviction, we must wrestle with ourselves until we come to basic beliefs that we will never surrender. As the years go on, we shall find that there are interpretations and conceptions about our faith that may change as we grow richer in understanding; but there can be no shifting of the main foundation. A building may have an extra story added on, a wing put here or there, new facing, new roofing, and interior alterations, but the foundation may not be tampered with safely.

The bedrock on which all of the preacher's convictions must be founded is a positive belief in God. Through the ages many have tried to state what they believe God to be. It may be of profit to look at a few of these conclusions:

Aristotle: the "Prime Mover"

Herbert Spencer: "The Infinite and Eternal Energy from which all things proceed"

Samuel Butler: "the Unknown"

H. G. Wells: the "Veiled Being"

A. N. Whitehead: the "Integral Impetus" or "Principle of Concretion" holding all "event particles" together in the orderly cosmos.[2]

Add to this list the thought of a writer on religion: God is *"the Inevitable Inference."*[3]

Despite the fact that each term has some truth in it, which one could be selected by a preacher as a foundational conviction that could be preached with compelling power? Surely, something more is needed, something with self-sustaining truth and eternal significance. Even though some of us may look askance at authoritative creeds, we may find guidance in the first paragraph of the Nicene Creed: "I believe in one God the Father Almighty, Maker of heaven and earth, and of all things visible and invisible. . . ." Here is a distillation of the Bible teachings about God: one, the Father, all-powerful, sole Creator. Directed by this, the preacher may come upon the beginning of a sturdy conviction concerning God; "For whoever would draw near to God must believe that he exists . . ."(Hebrews 11:6).

To stop here, however, would be as incomplete as if a man found a huge chunk of gold ore but never took it to the refiner. The preacher would not be able to preach of the hidden richness of his find inasmuch as that preciousness had not been uncovered. It is certain that those who would hear the preachings would not be moved by an exposition of the preacher's suppositions about God; they would want to hear of the preacher's current and constant experience of God.

The refinement of the conviction about God that will lead to a true and continuing experience of God will depend upon the preacher's belief concerning Jesus the Christ. The preacher must hear and answer the question asked by Jesus himself: "Who do you say that I am?" Those who knew Jesus at a distance had told the disciples that they believed him to be "one of the prophets." But Peter, who was Jesus' daily companion, said to him, "You are the Christ, the Son of the living God" (Matthew 16:14–16). Even today these two answers to the eternal question are being given by preachers. Each preacher must decide which way to choose. But if a preacher cannot give the answer of Peter, what is there to preach? G. K. Chesterton expressed this very well. Comparing other religions and other presentations of God with the Christ-centered message, he wrote:

But what the gods are supposed to *be*, what the priests are commissioned to *say*, is not a sensational secret like what those running messengers of the Gospel had to say. Nobody else except those messengers has any Gospel; nobody else has any good news; for the simple reason that nobody else has any news.[4]

Up until the time of Jesus, the world had repeatedly experienced birth, marriage, death, wars, famines, good times and bad times, the rise of philosophers, the appearances of religious leaders, sunrises and sunsets; none of this was news any more. But the apostles ran with news. God had come among men; he had died for their sins; he had risen from the dead! This was news then; it is news now. Out of his or her conviction of the truth of these statements, the preacher becomes the current amen sayer to these ideas. This, and this alone, becomes the preacher's message that has the power to change persons and to turn the world upside down.

Thus, the rough ore of the preacher's belief in God is refined by belief in Christ Jesus. And to complete the conviction, the preacher can believe that the Holy Spirit constantly irradiates the refined conviction and discloses its many facets and planes. The conviction becomes inexhaustible in its possibilities and beauty. Then the preacher can preach and preach without boredom or monotony. With confidence, the preacher may know that the preaching is not fruitless or in vain.

Hearers of the preaching may have the true God come into them until that gnawing emptiness in their souls, which they could not explain, is fully filled. The philosopher Pascal knew of this emptiness and said:

> . . . there was once in man a true happiness of which there now remain to him only the mark and empty trace, which he in vain tries to fill from all his surroundings. . . . But these are all inadequate, because the infinite abyss can only be filled by an infinite and immutable object, that is to say, only by God Himself.[5]

The preacher will become aware of the incompleteness of human lives from the news of world problems, crime, and despair reported in newspapers and on television. The things that are done and said in the world today would be vastly different if all persons had God within. How shall they find God to round out life and make it whole? The answer came centuries ago: "But how are men to call upon him in whom they have not believed? And how are they to believe in him of whom they have never heard? And how are they to hear without a preacher?" (Romans 10:14). A fourth question might be added: "And how are preachers to preach unless they themselves believe?"

Recently, during a state budget crisis, a job-training program for youths was being eliminated. A reporter from a TV station interviewed some of the young people as to the effect this might have on them. One girl said plaintively, "If we can't learn here, there *ain't nobody going nowhere.*" Without the guidance of those capable of teaching the job skills, *nowhere* would be the only destination for the seekers. They need those who have done the work and who know the best way of doing it as their teachers and inspirers. And thus it is with preaching. For those who do not know how to come to God, there must be preachers who have wrestled with their own doubts and who can now help others.

Having arrived, then, at some convictions about God so strong and convincing that the preacher has the same necessity to express them that moved Peter and John ("we cannot but speak of what we have seen and heard" [Acts 4:20]), he or she must formulate a belief about humankind. Faced with and confronted by the awesomeness of the universe and oneself, the preacher is bound to share the amazed wonder of David—"what is man that thou are mindful of him, and the son of man that thou dost care for him . . .?" (Psalm 8:4).

As was true when coming to personal convictions about God, the preacher will find that others have been before him or her seeking answers. Answers that have been put forth by some of these others needs to be evaluated:

The German philosopher Nietzsche: "The earth has a skin. That skin is full of sores. One of these sores is called man."[6]

Greek poet Homer: Man is "a leaf."

Greek poet Pindar: Man is "the dream of a shadow"[7]

French philosopher Pascal: "Man is but a reed, the feeblest thing in nature; but he is a reed that thinks."[8]

Greek proverb: "A *man* is a bubble."[9]

None of these come anywhere near the answer that came to David on a long-ago starry night. By the inspiration of God, surely, he knew what man is.

> Thou hast made him little less than God,
>   and dost crown him with glory and honor.
> Thou hast given him dominion over the works of thy hands;
>   thou hast put all things under his feet. . . .
>
> —Psalm 8:5-6

As a preacher ponders these things on the way to a strong conviction about humankind, it may help to remember that Jesus came in human form (reread Philippians 2:5-8). But the greatest directive of all is found in the fact that we are of such worth that our Lord considered us worth dying for. The conviction of this infinite and eternal worth will enable a preacher to look into the eyes of one person or into the eyes of the many individuals making up an audience or congregation and see, not shadows, feeble reeds, or pests, but potential "heirs of God and fellow heirs with Christ" (Romans 8:17). Belief in God and belief in a purposeful destiny for humankind run so closely together that a preacher will not be able to separate the strands.

Today, as at no other period in the history of humankind, people are desperate for the knowledge of themselves as being of greater significance than that assigned them by the world. A person resists being computerized into a statistic. To be reduced to a mere number—Social Security, bank account, insurance policy, credit card, and dozens of others—is a horribly cold existence. Surely to be here on this earth means more than to be a unit to be counted! If the preacher has come to a certainty about God's purpose for all men and women, young and old, including everyone in God's family, there is a life-changing message to preach.

If, then, the preacher has come to convictions about God and humankind that will stand the onslaughts of all foes, both spiritual and secular, what more is needed?

Put simply, a conviction is an answer to a question. Having felt the call to preach, the preacher-to-be has asked questions; painfully and slowly the convictions have come in reply. In turn, those persons who come to the preaching or who are found by the preacher will be asking questions. The core of the questions will be "Watchman, what of the night?" (Isaiah 21:11).

Those people in the night of doubt about the existence and nature of God will come to the preacher with their question. Having come to definite convictions about God, the preacher will be able to answer with joy and confidence, "Insofar as God is concerned, 'Morning comes . . .' (Isaiah 21:12)."

Those in the night of uncertainty concerning the reason and reality of humankind will come to the preacher with their question. Having come to a comforting and sure conviction about humankind, the preacher will be able, in this instance also, to speak strongly and without reservation, "'Morning comes. . . .'"

The preacher—the watchman on his watchtower—will have many other questions brought by inquirers about the night surrounding a person faring through this world.

"What about my sins? What about the things I have done and thought, yes, and continue to do and think, that are not in the will of God and that have injured me and others?" To answer this heart-rending and gnawing sense of guilt, the preacher must have convictions to share with others. Biblical teachings, especially the statements of Jesus, can lead the preacher to know about the preacher's own sins that are in the same category as those of any other person. It will also be helpful to observe how Jesus assured sinners: ". . . your sins are forgiven" (see, e.g., Matthew 9:2). And then there are the heartlifting words from God found in Isaiah 43:25,

> "I, I am He
> who blots out your trangressions for my own sake,
> and I will not remember your sins."

and in Psalm 103:12,

> as far as the east is from the west,
> so far does he remove our transgressions from us.

This truth John Bunyan showed us in his illustration in *Pilgrim's Progress* of Pilgrim making his way through life with difficulty, bearing a huge burden on his back. When he came to the cross, that burden fell off and Pilgrim walked the rest of his days in gladsome lightness of heart and mind. That heavy load represented his sins.

Along with this question of sin is bound to come the question about rewards and punishment, particularly the latter. The terms "heaven" and "hell" will come up. Here, again, the preacher must have a personal answer in order to give an answer to others. It is more than likely that no two preachers will hold exactly the same position of conviction at this point. Perhaps all will admit, however, the terribleness of sin, the poison of sin, and the death-dealing power of sin—"For the wages of sin is death" (Romans 6:23a). On the other side, those who humbly come to God will find that "the free gift of God is eternal life . . ." (Romans 6:23b).

With these two sides of the coin in mind, plus this truth from Matthew 19:25-26—". . . the disciples . . . [said], 'Who then can be saved?' But Jesus . . . said to them, 'With men this is impossible, but with God all things are possible'"—the preacher may work out a position on the separation of good and evil and whether or not that separation is eternal. The conclusion of contemporary theologian Hans Küng regarding Jesus' teachings about the forgiveness of sin may help: "Jesus did . . . forgive . . . all sins—except the sin against the Holy Spirit, against the reality of God himself, when the sinner does not want to be forgiven. Evidently an *opportunity* is offered to *everyone*. . . ."[10]

And there will be brought to the preacher many other questions (only a preacher will know how many) such as:

"What is the meaning of pain and suffering?"

"What about the Christian and violence and warfare?"

"What is a Christian view of marriage and divorce?"

The preacher will find that for some questions a conviction in the form of a guiding principle is the best that the Spirit will give. Not always can the answer be in such terms as "Thus saith the Lord" or "Definitely yes," or "Definitely no."

However, the purpose of this entire chapter is to stress the absolute necessity for the preacher to come to terms with the questions of life, reaching the point at which he or she can respond with a proclamation like a bugle sounding a mighty, unmistakable, rallying blast. The bugle is of no avail if it gives forth no more than a hesitant "beep"! (See 1 Corinthians 14:8.)

Finally (a word that might better be omitted by preachers!), the preacher's convictions must be the boundaries and salient points of a consistent life. This was well said by Carlyle, "But indeed Conviction, were it never so excellent, is worthless till it convert itself into Conduct. Nay, properly, Conviction is not possible till then. . . ."[11] Much of the preacher's preaching, much of the best of the preaching, is done without words.

4

Compassion

"Nobody knows the trouble I've seen. . . ."

These words from an old spiritual may well be repeated by any preacher who has been busy at the task of serving God for any length of time. Indeed, the preacher might go a bit further and point out that the majority of the troubles brought by needy people have been "trouble with a capital 'T'" as in the song from *The Music Man*. The preacher's task and position are such that he or she becomes a focus for the parish problems and difficulties. Our question here is, What is the preacher to do about these things? What can be done about them?

As we found in the preceding chapter, convictions are sealed and stamped "genuine" by the life conduct of the preacher. What the preacher soundly believes about God and persons must find a sincere expression when the preacher is faced by the life-laming conditions that beset those who come for help. The best and most comprehensive word that will serve as the statement of the preacher's attitude toward the manifold ills of humankind is "compassion." This word comes to us with the highest credentials:

> When he [Jesus] saw the crowds, he had *compassion* for them, because they were harassed and helpless, like sheep without a shepherd (Matthew 9:36, author's emphasis).

. . . a man who had died was being carried out, the only son of his mother, and she was a widow. . . . And when the Lord saw her, he had *compassion* on her and said to her, "Do not weep" (Luke 7:12-13, author's emphasis).

At this point it may be well to compare "compassion" and "sympathy." Translators of the Bible into English have consistently used "compassion" rather than "sympathy." Even though many dictionaries treat the two words as synonymous, there is something in the roots of "compassion" and its common usage that make it a more expressive word. Card stores may have a section marked "Sympathy Cards" but never one marked "Compassion Cards." Sympathy may lend itself to the polite and superficial. We may remember how, in Lewis Carroll's *Through the Looking Glass,* the walrus and the carpenter took the oysters for a long walk down the beach and how the oysters stopped and cried out that they were out of breath. In response, the walrus said, "I weep for you, I deeply sympathize." Then he and the carpenter ate all of the out-of-breath oysters. True compassion cannot be expressed by a card or a verbal statement. Compassion carries with it a great feeling for the afflicted and an active effort to help bear the load and relieve the pressure.

There is pressure where there is trouble, anguish, guilt, worry, bereavement, illness, or loss. The trouble can build up within the person like a head of steam with no safety valve, or like a great flood of water rising with no overflow outlet. Here the preacher's compassion may be exercised in a way to decrease the pressure and bring the harassed person back to a normal level of living appropriate to a child of God. A poet sensed this kind of compassionate response in the apostle Paul:

Desperate tides of the whole world's anguish
Forced thro' the channels of a single heart.[1]

When the sufferer can find no way to discharge the grief, then the preacher becomes the channel through which the accumulated woe flows out into an ocean of forgiveness and peace and love.

The preacher, however, as the channel, feels the force of whatever passes through. We understand that Jesus bore the sins of the whole world and that the cross was the result.

In fact, it is this flow of the world's anguish through the heart that supplies the preacher's titles, topics, and scriptural applications for sermons. Each person coming to hear the preaching has a personal tide of woe of some kind and listens for the word that will speak to that particular need. Ralph Waldo Emerson felt this as he sat in his pew one Sunday morning:

> "At church to-day I felt how unequal is this match of words against things. Cease, O thou unauthorized talker, to prate of consolation, resignation, and spiritual joys in neat and balanced sentences. For I know these men who sit below. Hush quickly, for care and calamity are *things* to them. There is the shoemaker whose daughter is gone mad, and he is looking up through his spectacles to see what you have for him. Here is my friend whose scholars are all leaving him, and he knows not where to turn his hand next. Here is the stage driver who has jaundice and cannot get well. Here is B, who failed last year, and he is looking up anxiously. Speak things or hold thy peace."[2]

Although the occupations mentioned are somewhat out-of-date, this admonition to the preacher speaks directly to the preacher of today whose hearers are grasped by the same kinds of difficulties and feelings of despair.

Indeed, if the preacher's heart is the channel through which the sorrows and troubles of the world are passing, the preacher must feel acutely a close identity with all troubled persons—even so far as to admit a joint ownership of the ills at hand. Then the preacher will be preaching to himself or herself and not *at* those who have come to be helped. Temptations to make sermons on pet themes, on a cleverly worked-out series, on intellectual overviews of prophecy, or on charismatic subjects will need to be subjected to the task at hand: Is this sermon likely to drain off the flooding tide of woes found here? Is this sermon an open and unclogged channel to the grace and mercy of God? Will there be felt in this preachment a pleading and sharing compassion rather than a beautifully turned word of sympathy? Is this truly a "we" sermon and not a "you" dissertation?

The preacher's compassion will be distinguished by its centering on each individual assailed by the trials of this life. There are times when the great need of the masses of people will bring forth a "blanket" type of compassion. However, even that overarching compassion will be of little value unless the preacher can single out one individual from the mass and see in that one person a representative of the whole, one whose want and despair can be multiplied to the total extent of the misery. We may well believe that when Jesus had compassion on the multitude, he did not lump the assembled people into a faceless crowd but knew that the great number could be broken down, and *must* be broken down, into units known as Samuel, David, Levi, Rachel, Mary, Anna, and many other distinct, struggling beings.

As a homely illustration of this person-directed compassion, we may think of a mother with a sick child. The doctor is called and treats the boy or girl as *a* patient. The doctor has many patients to see and to treat, but the mother has but one who will be her concern and care until the sick child's health returns. A preacher will not deal with a parish or a congregation, but with Bill and John and Susan and Laura. If the preacher succeeds in doing this, there will be those who say, on their way out of church, "Preacher, how did you know I needed that particular word this morning? You spoke directly to me." As difficult as it seems, the preacher needs to accept each soul under his or her guidance as near and dear, just as did the mother with the sick child.

Early in his preaching career, one preacher found the proof of this one-to-one preaching. A parishioner's wife was in a hospital and was being prepared for a serious operation. When the man had had his last few words with his wife before the nurses wheeled her down the hall to the operating room, he turned his tear-dimmed eyes to his pastor. That preacher took the man out onto the busy sidewalk in front of the hospital and walked him up and down for two hours while the surgery was in progress. His preaching for that man that day was a revelation to him of the infinite value of the personal touch.

After a long ministry of preaching, a preacher will be amazed at the nature of the dearest memories that are his or hers. Of course, there will be memories of times when congregations were swayed by the message and when the presence of the Spirit was undeniable. But ever so many of the memories will be of times when the preaching was quietly done with a man or woman or boy or girl in a crisis moment. Often crowds followed Jesus to hear his words, but also there were numerous times when he spoke to one person. All of this was preaching, proclamation of the kingdom.

Another manner in which the preacher's compassion comes to light is in the sharing of troubles and woes. Let us think of two news reporters describing battles being fought. One reporter does his work in an air-conditioned office in a luxurious office building in New York City. By means of electronic comunication he receives the facts of what is happening at a distance. He sits before a microphone and tells the world about the fierce conflicts, the loss of life, the destruction of property, the fate of refugees. The other reporter is on the field of battle. He is in the same line of fire as the soldiers. He eats whatever is available to the others. He may suffer wounds or lose all of his possessions.

These reporters illustrate the two ways a preacher has of gaining knowledge of what goes on in the lives of those whom he or she serves. Conferences, seminars, books, occasional field trips, and local surveys may add some useful information, but these sources cannot supply that which can be called firsthand experience.

The objection may be raised, however, that actual sharing of the specific sufferings of people is not always possible. Suppose that the preacher enjoys perfect health, how can he or she truly enter into the feelings of someone who must endure the pains of terminal cancer? Older people have been amused at times (and exasperated at times!) by the young and middle-aged "experts" on the problems of the aging. Is it possible for one to stand outside the body, mind, and spirit of another and do more than be a cheerleader or Job's comforter?

There is a way for the preacher to have such a close communion with those who need comfort that the anguish of one will flow into the other. We have used a mother as an illustration, and we know from experience that when a child is in pain or difficulty, the parent suffers even though the disease or error is in the child. If there is a sincere desire to share, compassion can find a way. A number of years ago a man felt so keenly the plight and oppression of black people (he was white) that he had his face and hands stained until he could pass for black. He went to live among the blacks of his community, and he received, at the hands of white people, the same treatment that the blacks had been receiving for generations. He could not become a black, but he found a way of sharing. In the same way, compassion will enable a preacher to identify with the ills of God's troubled children. The limits of this sharing will be determined by the intensity of the compassion.

Ezekiel was directed of God to this kind of sharing: "The Spirit lifted me up and took me away . . . and I came to the exiles at Telabib, who dwelt by the river Chebar. *And I sat there overwhelmed among them seven days*" (Ezekiel 3:14-15, author's emphasis). By the aid of the Spirit we, as preachers, can pour out our hearts in our messages because we have sat where the unfortunate are sitting.

We are seeing how the concept of compassion grows as we examine it carefully. Another aspect may be called that of the "outstretched hand." Austin Phelps sensed this and expressed the need clearly:

> The Master walking on the sea in the night, and stretching forth his hand to the sinking Peter, is the emblem of that which a Christian preacher must be in every age, if he would speak to real conditions, and minister to exigent necessities.[3]

The compassion called for here is not for physical or mental troubles as much as it is for the struggle of the spirit. In the story of that night on the water, we may find the symbols that will match what we find all around us today. Peter was afloat on a tempestuous sea, but he had underneath him what seemed the most solid thing he could find for his trip through the waters. So it is with persons unrelated to the Christ. They have certain beliefs and practices that they may have inherited or found, and they are going through life not at all sure that they will make it to the other side but not knowing any better way to function. Then Peter caught a glimpse of Jesus and wanted to go to him. In this same way hearers of the Word experience an urge when they are confronted by the Savior. Peter left his seemingly solid ship and started out toward Jesus; but then he began to sink. What courage it takes for anyone to leave old, familiar beliefs and try for better! And the newfound faith often proves insufficient. At the moment of sinking Peter may have said to himself, "Oh, why did I leave the safety of the boat?" And then the hand of Christ reached out, and Peter took his place with his Lord. In our time as preachers we are ordained to follow Jesus' example and stretch forth a hand to all seekers who are finding the going rough.

So far we have marveled at how hard is the task of a preacher, and now we are reminded again that ours is never an easy task. In every congregation there may be some who are at the Peter stage—finding it hard to come to complete commitment to Jesus and yet having left the old beliefs. In the sermon there must be something of a helping hand for all such. Looked at closely, there may be but few in the congregation who do not need this kind of helping hand for reinforcement as the waves of modern life and thinking swirl about them.

One thing that we might bear in mind as we prepare to preach the compassion of the helping hand is, in the words of W. H. Auden, that we should not be "lecturing on navigation while the ship is going down."[4]

Compassion is not, however, concerned exclusively with feeling with the sufferer and letting that person know that there is one who senses how hard the situation is. There are many times when true compassion will be shown as interpretation of the ills being borne. Pain, misfortune, and failure are never welcome guests, but if something good can be gained from them, they need never be life-shattering. A compassionate preacher may be able to show one profit from the dark spots—growth.

The writer was blessed with an old-fashioned grandmother who was not abreast of the teachings and findings concerning adolescence. She did not know the fancy terms for the physical and emotional changes going on within the body and "psyche" of her teenaged grandson. The word "trauma" was not in her vocabulary. And when the grandson was moody, rebellious, or insecure, she comforted him with these words of wisdom: "All you've got is *growing pains.* And pretty soon your growing pains will be over and you will be a *man!*" A homely but sound and true philosophy!

The preacher can find much in the Bible to season sermons on the eternal truth that growth of the spirit can be the grand result of many trials in the process of living. After the trials, indeed in the midst of them, a mature Christian can emerge. Said Paul, ". . . we rejoice in our sufferings, knowing that suffering produces endurance, and endurance produces character, and character produces hope . . ." (Romans 5:3-4).

In one of his sonnets the artist-poet Michelangelo tells the story of a woman who visited his studio and was grieved to see him attack a beautiful piece of marble with hammer and chisel until the chips were flying in a veritable shower. She remonstrated with the sculptor that he was spoiling the beauty of the lovely stone. Michelangelo replied: "The more the marble wastes, the more the statue grows." We can show that, by God's good grace, the more we are losing and enduring in this world, the more our likeness to the pattern of Christ will be seen.

So we see that a preacher's compassion is a many-pronged thing; it is expressed in several ways and will be tempered by the sight of the need at hand. But we should beware lest we think we have achieved a permanent and unconquerable spirit of compassion. Often we shall be weary of the struggle. We shall come to be impatient with some who lean on us too heavily; we shall be disillusioned by some who make a profession of misfortune. All of this will come in our preaching career, and we shall need to refer more and more to the example of Jesus. We shall need to walk with him again and again as he made his way among the same kind of people and never failed to love them all and feel compassion for them in their various needs.

We shall know that we are at least approaching compassion when we can consider all of the more than four billion people in the world and long to be of help to each one. A writer had such a feeling when he was thumbing through a huge telephone directory:

> A million hearts here wait our call,
> All naked to our distant speech:
> I wish that I could ring them all
> And have some welcome news for each. [5]

5

Hope

What have we done so far?

Inadvertently, it would seem that we have followed the classical sermon form—three points! We have dealt with the cross, conviction, and compassion—the mighty three Cs of preaching. We know that a three-point sermon always has subpoints, but so mighty are the considerations of the cross, conviction, and compassion that it would seem that all possible subpoints of a lifetime of preaching are gathered up and that no more need be said. However, there are some subjects that just cry out for additional study. One of these, which we are to examine now, is *hope*.

First of all we are faced with what has confronted us in the other aspects of preaching, namely the necessity of the preacher's having his or her own reservoir of the quality he or she is endeavoring to give to others. A preacher who hopes to instill hope in the hearts of hearers must have a heart well stocked with hope. This is a "must," but it is not the easiest qualification to come by. As we have observed, the preacher becomes the channel of the woes of others, including the hopelessness in the lives of today's people. The preacher is not dealing, then, with a diluted despair but with a concentrate of hopelessness. Rising above this to the point of being able to infuse every sermon with Paul's triumphant note—"Rejoice, and again I say to you rejoice" (Philippians 4:4)—is not possible except by a gift from God.

The point is that a preacher will spend so many hours in hospitals, nursing homes, undertakers' establishments, courts of law, and homes where domestic strife or catastrophes have torn the fabric of purposeful living, that he or she will always understand hope as a conditioned asset. The effect of this constant moving in a milieu where people are holding onto hope by a slender thread or have given up hope completely was reflected in the private life of a certain preacher. A member of his church came to visit in the parsonage and was looking over the records and tapes on a music stand. In surprise, he remarked to his pastor, "Why, almost everything here is in a minor key!" Perhaps that preacher had not been aware that his selections reflected the pervasive sadness that had come from suffering with others. Sinking into this kind of despondency undermines the preacher's ability to lift others to the plane of hope available to every child of God.

This familiarity with the hopelessness of many not only may result in an underlying sadness but may produce a protective callousness on a preacher's sensitivity. A young preacher encountered this when he went to serve a church in a resort town. After having been there for a few months, he was filled with enthusiasm for the possibility of interchurch cooperation in a campaign to reach every inhabitant. He shared his idea with the other ministers and received varied responses. Then he approached the one who had been in the town longer than any of the others. This preacher listened politely and then said, "Young man, when you have been here as long as I have, you will no longer give a hoot." (Confidentially, the preacher did not use the word "hoot"!) In all justice to this seemingly hard-bitten preacher, it was more than possible that his callousness was the accumulated result of valiant battles against hopelessness in his parish and parsonage that had ended in apparent defeat. Cardinal Manning expressed this situation when he said, "Forty years of preaching often look like forty years of beating the air."[1] We note, however, that he was not ready to admit defeat; he specifically said that his efforts "often *look like* . . ." (author's emphasis). The preacher who possesses hope can see hope even in times and occasions when no visible victories can be counted.

We look at the reasons why a preacher may face every person and every situation in the world with an inner fortification of hope. In the first place we are servants of a God of hope and not a God of hopelessness: "May the God of hope fill you with all joy and peace in believing, so that by the power of the Holy Spirit you may abound in hope" (Romans 15:13). God gave to Abram the hope of a city beyond his wanderings, gave to Moses and the Israelites the hope of the Promised Land after their years of slavery, gave to David the hope of a dynasty with implications beyond the present kingdom, and, finally, gave to every contrite seeker the hope of a new birth through God's Son.

A second base for our hope is described by the old saying (so old that it was used as early as 170 B.C.) "While there's life, there's hope." Jesus' constant emphasis was on life, such as, "'I am the way, and the truth, and the life'" (John 14:6*a*) and "'I came that they may have life, and have it abundantly'" (John 10:10*b*). We are called to announce that there can be no hopelessness here since there is a future life grounded in the eternal God. This life is eternal and, therefore, hope is eternal.

Thus, the preacher fares forth with an unassailable hope that can be offered to all. Until the preacher is absolutely sure of this personal hope, it would be tragic to try to lift others out of the "Slough of Despond." If the preacher has one foot in that slough, there is small chance for him or her to be the rescuer of another who is entangled there.

This conviction of hope on the part of the preacher does not mean, however, that the preacher will be so naive as to expect that the world is just filled to the brim with joy and gladness! Quite the contrary. Apart from a hope founded in God, people will tend to have a volatile kind of hope that is dependent upon the ups and downs of the days and years. These persons are like someone who has money invested in the stock market. He or she may have an entire life savings tied up in five different stocks. At the close of each market day this investor will look anxiously at the figures that indicate whether the stocks have gone up or down since the last report. During twenty-four hours the total amount of the savings might be cut in half, and some days it is possible for all of the savings to dwindle to nothing. There will be times of elation and times of deadly despair. So it is with those who do not have a firm hope based on trust in God. Their investments may be in children, a career, a house, some dream of a secure future, the integrity of a friend, good health, national peace, a stable economy, and so forth. If circumstances damage or destroy or diminish the life they have invested in one or more of these, they do not have a sure hope that can ride out the losses and storms. To these persons the preacher holds out hope that is much more than the encouragement to "hang in there; things are bound to improve!" No, the preacher offers hope *plus*—hope plus joy: "Happy is he whose help is the God of Jacob, whose hope is in the LORD his God" (Psalm 146:5).

In addition to the changes and losses that come to people and cause them to lose hope as the perfect life they had envisioned becomes less and less possible, the preacher will find that the total weight of the disappointments will result in an attitude of "What's the use? I work and sacrifice and do without and try to be a good person, and what do I achieve after all?" This hollowness will not seem strange to a preacher because the preacher has felt the same temptation to lose heart. The writer has found a good illustration of this empty feeling in the experience of poet Sidney Lanier. This poet had tuberculosis, and in his day the only treatment thought to be effective was sun and fresh air. So it happened, one day, that Lanier was stretched out in a field of clover. The sun shone upon him and the gentle breeze touched his cheek and he had a sense of joy. To while away the time he began to think of some of the people who had passed through this world and had made a contribution that had added to his well-being. He thought of the poet Keats, the musician Beethoven, the artist Raphael, the playwright Shakespeare, and others who had made his life richer. Fancifully, he se-

lected certain stems of clover and named each one for these men
and others in his memory. He was pleased to think himself in the
company of such gifted people. Just then, a farmer's brawny ox
came into the field to munch the clover. At length the animal came
to "Keats," "Beethoven," and the rest—and ate them all.! Indig-
nantly, Lanier wrote:

> So: they have played their part.
>   and to this end?
> This, God? This, troublous-breeding Earth? This, Sun
> Of hot, quick pains? To this no-end that ends,
> These Masters wrought, and wept, and sweated blood,
> And burned, and loved, and ached with public shame,
> . . . This was all? This Ox?[2]

The ox to Lanier was the symbol of the "Course-of-things"—
that ongoing life took all of the work that was done by the men
and women in the world. This end result seemed to him a waste of
all good workmanship. But then he seemed to hear his admired
men of the arts saying:

> Nay, . . .
> God's clover, we, and feed His Course-of-things;
> The pasture is God's pasture; . . .
> The general brawn is built for plans of His. . . .[3]

This fancied answer of the eminent persons in the poem is the
answer of hope that God gives to the preacher, who, in turn, gives
it to others. The preacher may think, at times, that an unresponsive
congregation—which seems not to be moved by the labor of love,
the anguish of seeking the guidance of the Spirit, and all else that
goes into a sermon—is like an ox chomping at all in its path without
pausing to savor one stem of clover as superior to any other! But
the preacher will learn that each member of the congregation also
has some brawny ox that devours his or her day's work, year's
work, or lifetime's work. The message of hope is that each one
contributes to the strength of the general purpose that God is
fostering in the world.

Indeed, even Paul came across the hungry oxen that feed on all
that is said and done and leave the pasture seemingly bare. He

names some of them—death, life, angels, principalities, things present, things to come, powers, height, depth. But, he says, none of these "will be able to separate us from the love of God" (Romans 8:38, 39). The preacher has the sure knowledge that nothing that is done worthily before God can be wasted. How sorely do the people of this age need that message of hope! Perhaps Jesus sums up this assurance of hope in this verse: "And whoever gives to one of these little ones even a cup of cold water because he is a disciple, truly, I say to you, he shall not lose his reward" (Matthew 10:42).

Another area of hopelessness that needs clearing is the individual's sense of personal failure to reach a desired goal. This goal was set on the assumption that the person had infinite possibilities within. Others might be born to end in obscurity or mediocrity—but not he or she! The British writer Boreham notes this human sense of inner greatness and appraises it in a rather quaint metaphor: "Man invariably sees things through the golden haze of futurity. . . . To himself he is always the *tadpole of an archangel*" (author's emphasis). [4] The point is that each one of us believes, at least to some extent, that within us is an embryo that may develop into a statesman, an artist, a writer, a power-wielding executive, an inventor, a skilled physician, a renowned preacher—something at top level in the world. Because of that belief an ambitious goal is set.

Family, friends, and teachers may help keep alive the innate assurance that we can and must reach the great goal. The success standard of the world contributes to the driving necessity of "being somebody."

But as years go on, a tragically high proportion of the people who have felt greatness stirring within themselves and who have launched out into life, never doubting that large achievement is around the corner, come far short of the goal. Thus the hopelessness of failure sets in. The person feels not only that he or she has failed to nurture the "tadpole" to "archangel" status but also that he or she has let down those who have trusted and waited and watched. The person also feels that the world at large is missing what might have been a real service to all people. So widespread is this kind of hopelessness that the preacher will find in this area of need one of the greatest fields of service.

Perhaps the primary truth to stress is that every person does have, as a gift of God, the "tadpole," the embryo, the possibility of noble development. It is not a mistake for anyone to feel the beginning of greatness moving within him or her. To be born in the image of God is an absolute assurance of the material of greatness.

However, the error comes from accepting the worldly standard of what constitutes the realization of one's God-given potential. To the world, the people listed in the *Who's Who* books are the winners Not so with God. In fact, the world's applause of a person rarely coincides with God's approval of that person.

The preacher will find the Bible rich in examples of persons who have started out on the road to fulfillment, marked out as the customary route for ambitious people, but who have had to change roads in order to reach God's goal for them.

There was Abram, who left Ur and the prescribed round of activity that promised him respect and prominence and started off toward a strange goal called "a city not made with hands." He eventually reached God's goal for him, which was to be the father of a great nation out of which would come, in human form, our Savior.

There was Joseph, the spoiled and pampered, who must have felt the bitterness of losing out on his growing position of authority when he languished in an Egyptian jail and worked as a slave for Potiphar. However, he was actually on his way to the goal of saving the lives of his people.

There was Moses, who might have been king of Egypt but who found himself out in the desert caring for cattle and living in a primitive way. He was on the way to God's goal for him, which was to deliver his people from bondage and into the Promised Land.

There was Esther, who risked death or forfeiture of a queen's privileges to speak for her people, but she was on the way to God's goal for her as the rescuer of her people.

The preacher will find many other subjects for sermons on this in both Testaments. Paul might have been another Gamaliel in his nation, or he might have been noticed by the Romans as a man fitted for a government post—except for the fact that he was put in the way of God's goal for him. John and James were possible heirs to a fishing business, and Levi was a prosperous tax official.

As good as any illustration, or perhaps even better, might be the preacher's own experience of dreaming of some other career, which offered more prestige and monetary reward.

If the preacher can be used of the Spirit to bring to hopeless people the comfort of knowing that they are not merely stragglers by the wayside while others are going on to acclaim and fortune and that they are fulfilling their best potential when they make God's goal for them their own goal, a mighty work will be done.

The preacher need not neglect the preaching of hope in the future, just because someone has derided the "pie in the sky" idea. As a matter of fact, hope cannot be a present concept. Hope is always a looking forward; as Paul said, "Now hope that is seen is not hope. For who hopes for what he sees?" (Romans 8:24). All the promises of God point to the future here and hereafter. We may preach boldly that no one of us is a static individual caged in this troubled and troubling world but that each of us is a pilgrim on God's highway going somewhere. This movement with and toward God means that all that would fill us with hopelessness is being left behind step after step.

Along with this positive message of the future joy in the kingdom, the preacher stresses the moment-by-moment attitude of hope coming to all children of God. We can show that hopelessness indicates that we doubt the invincibility of our Lord. And hopelessness indicates a feeling of aloneness, whereas Jesus assured us, ". . . lo, I am with you always, to the close of the age" (Matthew 28:20).

As a closing thought on our dealings with hopelessness, is it not fair to say that we preachers must never share in any sort of abject hopelessness? Is not the whole content of the Gospel that we have

to proclaim against this attitude? How can we admit hopelessness
and then go out with a good conscience to cry out our belief in
the being, the worth and work, the everlasting love of our Almighty, Creator-Redeemer God? No matter what we see of evil
and injustice in the world, no matter what are the threats of war
and the indications of ecological disaster, our authority is such that
we are made able to look hopelessness in the face and say, as
Shakespeare made Northumberland say:

> . . . even through the hollow eyes of death
> I spy life peering. . . .[5]

6

Love

"Love the people—love the people—love the people," said the seminary professor with all the fervor that he could muster. "When you get out into your churches, forget, if you will, all that I have taught about the English Bible, but never forget what I am saying to you now—love the people!"

No better advice could have been given to that class of preachers-in-training, and no better advice can be given to preachers at any time. If a preacher aspires to work with God in the making of saints, in the building of the kingdom, in the fashioning of a new and better world, people will be the material out of which these creations are to come. Other workmen will have to do with insensate raw materials, but the preacher always will be restricted to one ingredient—people.

For this reason the preacher must heed the exhortation of the professor, for only by love can people be moved to be a part of the divine creative purpose of God.

Not so with the craftsmen working with other materials. The potter need not love the clay that is kneaded and pulled and shaped and fired. Indeed, in the process of turning a bowl or a vase on the potter's wheel, much of the clay is removed. The potter may love the finished product without caring at all for the clay that was necessary to make it.

And the sculptor has the same freedom toward the marble or other material that is used for a statue or figurine. The stone may be chipped and pounded and cut, with much of the stone going into the trash pile. The sculptor's desire is for the work of art to emerge from the block of material.

The carpenter, also, need have no affection for the wood that is used. Without any regret whatsoever, the carpenter will saw, chisel, hammer, plane, sand, and paint the wood. The carpenter has in mind a cabinet, a chair, or even a house. This is illustrated by the story of a builder mentioned in one of the *Foxfire* books. When a visitor came to town, this man would point out a schoolhouse that he had built some years ago. He did not mention the bricks or planks or iron railings; it was the *schoolhouse* that was his pride and joy.

How different, then, is the method of the preacher! Only by loving the material at hand—the people—can the preacher hope to have any completed "kingdom segment" or work-in-process at the end of the day.

Opposed to the preacher's love approach, which is a difficult and disciplining task, is the world's evaluation of the preacher's "material." In the world the people will be called "troops" by the military, "hands" by factory owners, "population" by the government, and "numbers" by computers. There was a time, and how far away it seems now, when a geographical place might be listed as a "town of three hundred *souls*." We do not hear that expression now. The precious building material of the preacher is categorized in the world according to the particular purpose of the person or agency doing the naming. Thus, to understand this matter of loving the people, the preacher needs to review the matter from two angles.

The first viewpoint is the preacher's own. Unfortunately, or perhaps fortunately, the people who come for the preacher's ministration will not all be easily lovable, darling, dear little old ladies! In fact, more than a few through the years will fall into the class of "pains in the neck," and yet they all must be loved without pretense or hypocrisy. The preacher must not face this love with a grimace and a reluctant acceptance of it as "a Christian duty." This was the approach of an official in a church who avoided crossing the path of another member. The pastor took the official to task and asked him, point-blank, "Do you or do you not love your Christian brother John Smith?" The answer was "Oh, yes, Pastor, I love him all right, *but I just can't stand him!*" But does not love mean the acceptance of a person and that person's presence? People hungry for love are to be loved as they are and not for some fancied projection of beauty and worth that is not theirs! Cromwell expressed this to Lely, the portrait painter who had come to put his likeness on canvas. He demanded that the artist not flatter him, but paint him as he was, "warts and everything."

Perhaps if love is looked at from the angle of demonstration, it will not seem so impossible. That same official who had such an aversion to John Smith was riding up to the floor of his office one bitterly cold morning and noticed a poorly clad messenger boy riding with him. He inquired of the lad, "Where is your coat? It is too cold to go out like that." Sullenly the boy answered, "I don't have a coat." And the man took off his own coat and wrapped it around the boy and said, "There—now you have a coat." If his pastor had asked the man, "Did you do that because you loved the boy?" he would have replied, "Love him? Why I never saw him before!" His action was love without analysis or recognized emotion. Seeing love in this way, a preacher can begin to understand how he or she can truly love even those who lean too heavily at times, who say the wrong things, who criticize, who block new approaches in the work of the church. Love begins by caring.

The preacher will learn that those in the congregation who burden him or her with the heaviest loads or with seemingly unimportant trifles are doing to the preacher what the preacher is doing to God. If the preacher will review the prayers of the day, the examination may well show that he or she has leaned heavily on the heavenly Father and that some of the petitions may, when compared to the greatness and majesty of God's ongoing work in the world, seem as trifles. And yet, the preacher is simply responding to the divine invitation.

> Cast your burden on the LORD,
> and he will sustain you. . . .
> —Psalm 55:22

"Cast all your anxieties on him, for he cares about you" (1 Peter 5:7). The people, hearing the preacher use these texts and considering the preacher as God's local representative, feel free to bring themselves and their life concerns. The preacher must learn that love is expressed by heartfelt caring. Those who come will sense whether or not the caring touches the preacher. During the presidential campaign of 1980, one of the candidates addressed a group of black leaders. He spoke most eloquently and persuasively. Afterward, however, one of the black women said, touching her lips, "He has it here," and then touching her heart, "But not here."

In addition to showing caring, the preacher can express love by an acceptance of responsibility for those who come. The age-old question "Am I my brother's keeper?" (Genesis 4:9) never ceases its echoing in the world. And the answer today is negative more often than positive. *Self*-fulfillment, *self*-improvement, and *self*-discovery take the place of being concerned about the sister or brother. For the preacher, however, being the sister's or brother's keeper is one of the chief justifications for preaching.

The preacher becomes a part of a group or congregation of which he or she is the center. The aim must be that expressed by Jesus, speaking of the twelve disciples: "While I was with them, I kept them in thy name, which thou hast given me; I have guarded them, and none of them is lost but the son of perdition . . ." (John 17:12). This is love expressed in responsibility. The ones given to the preacher by God are to be shepherded carefully through this wolf-infested world.

We have seen this responsibility in operation in camps that have swimming as part of the program. An older boy or girl is assigned a younger boy or girl as a "buddy." The older person must go into the water with the younger and not be content until that one comes safely out of the water. Colleges may utilize this method by using upper-class students as "big brothers" or "big sisters." In either instance the charge is accepted voluntarily, just as a preacher accepts the oversight of a congregation. The very acceptance is an assumption of unremitting responsibility.

Love, also, is expressed by respect. But to whom do we give respect in the world? Is it not to persons who have proved themselves by notable achievement in a chosen field of work, to persons who have made for themselves a position in life that is worthy, to persons who bear well an honored name, to persons of integrity and excellent character, to persons who are clean and self-supporting? In other words, we respect persons whose values we share. How, then, can a preacher find it possible to give respect to all of those who have become his or her responsibility? Among a hundred people would there not be a number who do not measure up to the standards of respectability that we have learned to follow? But if the preacher is to love the people, there must be respect even for the last and the least in the congregation. How, then?

A good start in this direction is to remember, again, that each person has something of the image of God. Just as monarchs of old were accustomed to giving a subject some article from the king's person to take along on a lengthy mission, which he could then show in order to be accorded respect and aid, so has God sent each of us into the world with something of himself. It is that "something" that commands of us respect for every person bearing it. Roman citizenship had much the same effect. When Paul, thought to be a wrongdoer, was about to be beaten, he announced that he was a freeborn Roman citizen. Even though the governor and soldiers did not change their opinion of his possible guilt, he was treated with respect and was not flogged.

Respect may come, also, from the fact of family relationship. Under God we are all one family (note Ephesians 3:14, 15 and Matthew 6:9-15, the Lord's Prayer). At one time, when President Carter's brother had done something that was threatening to compromise the president, Jimmie was reported to have said, "He is my brother, and I love him." When a preacher accepts all those under his or her pastoral care as brothers and sisters, there is love and respect.

Another approach to love by the preacher comes through knowledge of the person involved. How well do we really know the persons who come, publicly or privately, to hear our proclamation of the gospel? Sometimes we may blame this on the inarticulateness of these seekers; they cannot get across to us their inner motives, and so there is no real communication. But is it not possible for there to be an inarticulateness of our understanding? It is only through the eyes of love that we can bridge the gap between us.

In reference to this difficulty of knowing what some other person is thinking and living by, Robert Louis Stevenson wrote an essay called "The Lantern Bearers." He used as an illustration a game he and his friends used to play. Each of them would obtain a small, enclosed lantern known as a "bull's-eye." At night each boy would light his lantern, hide it under his coat, and walk across the fields to a meeting place. Once there, with the doors of their hiding place closed, the boys would disclose their lanterns. On the way, however, anyone who happened to pass a boy would have no idea that he carried a secreted lantern or why he was intent on walking in one direction so determinedly. Stevenson uses this illustration to show that each person goes through the world with his or her particular lantern—a driving life force—that determines acts and direction. But the lantern of the chief motive in each life is hidden from others. For this reason we classify others as strange, odd, miserly, unorthodox, hostile, maladjusted, and so forth. Stevenson concludes that as a man is seen by another,

> His life from without may seem but a rude mound of mud; there will be some golden chamber at the heart of it, in which he dwells delighted; and for as dark as his pathway seems to the observer, he will have some kind of a bull's-eye at his belt.[1]

In love, the preacher needs to become so well acquainted with the people that it is possible to fathom the inner urge that really represents the person.

We have looked at some possible entries of love as the preacher yearns over the people to be served in God's name. Now we turn from the preacher's viewpoint to that which may seem to us to be God's viewpoint. How did, how does, God express love toward us?

For one thing, we know that God exhibited love in divine sharing. In older books of theology the "attributes" of God are confidently and sometimes rather arbitrarily listed. But how is it that we feel free to say that God is this or that? These intimations that have come to be part of our conception of God must have come from God's sharing with us in one way or another. We speak of God as being holy, true, loving, unchangeable; we speak of God as just, righteous, all-knowing, all-powerful, ever present; we call God "heavenly Father." Why?

Why, because God in love has shared the knowledge of the divine in the beauty we see on earth and in the sky, in the words of men and women inspired by the Spirit, in the highest aspirations of the persons around us, and by the glimmerings of these attributes in our own gropings toward that which is lovely and of good report. As Paul said to the people of Lystra, ". . . he did not leave himself without witness, for he did good and gave you from heaven rains and fruitful seasons, satisfying your hearts with food and gladness" (Acts 14:17).

With this example of love, the preacher may sense how necessary it is that he or she share of self with the people. In his poem "The Preacher's Mistake," the poet Brewer Mattocks told of a preacher who climbed up into the church steeple and stayed there. He meditated and waited for God's word to come. Every day he wrote part of a sermon, and twice a week he dropped the written sermon down on the heads of the people! Is it not likely that people treated in that fashion would wonder about the man so high above them and discuss among themselves, "What is he really like? Does he feel tempted at all? Does he have any pain? Does he laugh at all? Does he see any beauty anywhere?"

Of this man, we preachers of today may be tempted to exclaim, "How very stupid!" But if we are honest, we may think of times when we stood aloof and more or less dropped our "wonderful" sermons on the heads of our people! To share self in love is to expose oneself to the people so that they may see how very much like them we are! As Paul and Barnabas said to the people who took them for gods, "We also are men, of like nature with you . . ." (Acts 14:15).

I remember that as a teenager I was sitting in church one Sunday morning when the preacher came into the pulpit at the last moment, flushed and agitated. Before beginning the service, he confessed, "Our home was greatly upset this morning. The cat took a fit and littered the house and climbed the curtains and tore them. . . ." Running his hand through his hair he went on, "Please bear with me; let us pray." Strangely enough, after all the years that have passed, the remembrance is that that day's sermon is more meaningful to me than many another. Other listeners expressed the same reaction. Was it that we knew then that the preacher was also a vulnerable person, just as we are? Sharing with the people one's own liability to the changes and misfortunes of life will be a sure symbol of mutual trust and love.

But more was needed from God than signs and seasons and words. These left multitudes unmoved. What more could and did God do to assure that we earthly children could have no doubt of God's love? A seventeenth-century mystic, Henry Scougal, has expressed God's act in a telling fashion:

> I remember one of the poets hath an ingenious fancy to express the passion wherewith he found himself overcome after a long resistance; that the god of love had shot all his golden arrows at him, but could never pierce his heart, till at length he put himself into the bow, and darted himself straight into his breast."[2]

God's final act of love was the gift of Jesus Christ.

With the preacher, also, nothing less than the gift of the whole self is going to convince the people of unquestioning love. Professionalism will not do; the personal perspective is indispensable.

One more thing may be said about the preacher wrapping all preachments in love.

God has shown that the foundation of all commandments is love. When a lawyer came to Jesus to inquire, "Teacher, which is the great commandment in the law?" the Lord telescoped all of the requirements that God has stated for earthly children into these few words: "You shall *love* the Lord your God with all your heart, and with all your soul, and with all your mind. . . . You shall *love* your neighbor as yourself" (Matthew 22:37-39, author's emphasis).

The preacher can do no more and no less. As the sermons open up the way to life and mark out the guideposts on the way (known as "commandments"), love must be the foundation of all the exhortations and warnings.

For the preacher, the thirteenth chapter of First Corinthians is an inviolable creed.

7

The Earthen Vessel

Lord, how can man preach thy eternal word?
He is a brittle crazy glass,
Yet in thy temple thou dost him afford
This glorious and transcendent place
To be a window, through thy grace.[1]

How well this poet, George Herbert of the seventeenth century, states our awesome situation as preachers! Assessing the situation from the human viewpoint, we cannot possibly transmit God's Holy Word to others; God achieves a miracle by making us the messengers of his gospel, despite our limitations.

Perhaps Paul was the first to realize fully this sobering and humbling condition of us as preachers: "But we have this treasure in earthen vessels, to show that the transcendent power belongs to God and not to us" (2 Corinthians 4:7). Both George Herbert and Paul point to a truth that may be hard for us to accept. The preacher is not the center of the initiation of the message; the preacher is the line of delivery. The life-sustaining fluid that flowed along the ancient aqueducts to provide cities with water did not ooze forth from the masonry of the conduits but came gushing from a lake, a giant spring, or other fountainhead in the hills. The healing solution that is dispensed through a hypodermic needle does not originate in the plastic, rubber, or glass of the syringe but has been placed there by a physician. The aqueduct and the syringe are "earthen vessels," without promise of producing *of themselves* the essentials to life.

At this point it may be well to clarify the thought expressed in order not to encourage poor work habits. Some of us might be ready to say: "See, study and long preparation are not only unnecessary but something of an affront to God. We need only to go into the pulpit on Sunday and speak whatever is given to us at the moment!" Not so. Not every chunk of marble scattered on the landscape delivered water to a city. Only the carefully squared stones that were deliberately and securely put into place did the job. There was nothing haphazard or spontaneous about the task of the component parts of the aqueduct. This is also true of the hypodermic needle; to serve its end, all parts of it have to be fastened together well and the whole thing kept sterile. By long hours and struggle the preacher prepares to be the "aqueduct" or the "syringe" as the occasion requires and is constantly ready for the precious water of life, God's instruction in righteousness, to flow through him or her.

The fact that we have been chosen from among so many others to administer the riches of the faith does not infer that we are being severed from our earthly origin. We are now, and always will be, of the same substance as our fellows who were not chosen for this exalted task. Their human weaknesses are our weaknesses; their temptations are our temptations. In us is working the process of deterioration, the built-in temporary quality of all persons. This circumstance of being earthen vessels may not wear upon us so much if we recognize that we are not expected to be "Christ's vicars on earth," as some ecclesiastics assume, but simply messengers—apostles. The remembrance of our true function will aid in keeping us from the tragedy of making the vicar more important in our preaching than the Christ whom we are to proclaim. It is recorded that Innocent III, after having been elected Pope at the young age of thirty-seven, "preach[ed] his consecration sermon simply about himself."[2] Although we may not confine ourselves to talking about ourselves exclusively, there is a real temptation to intrude our own affairs, dislikes, desires, prejudices, and ambitions into sermons. At such times it will help to remember that we are, at best, earthen vessels that must not color or contaminate the treasure entrusted to us.

This brings to mind another error that we may make. Being so close to the treasure of the gospel for so long a time, we may eventually alter our "earthen vessel" aspect until we begin to believe that we are like the Word we preach. We like the stories of how the *stigmata*—the marks of Christ's wounds—appeared on St. Francis of Assisi and a few others. The reason given for the appearance of the marks was that these persons lived so close to the Lord that they became like him. To our joy, we always have the possibility of improvement as the Spirit accompanies us year after year. However, if we have the confident hope that gradually we shall work out of the "earthen" classification, it would be well for us to look again at the experience of Peter and Paul. Peter, directly, and Paul, by vision, were closer to the Savior than we are likely to be in this world. And yet Peter denied the Lord three times after having been with him day after day for nearly three years; and Paul, after the wonderful vision on the road to Damascus, found it necessary to admit: ". . . I do not do the good I want, but the evil I do not want is what I do. . . . For I delight in the law of God in my inmost self, but I see in my members another law at war with the law of my mind and making me captive to the law of sin which dwells in my members" (Romans 7:19, 22-23).

But if we as preachers are tempted to bewail our designation as earthen vessels and aspire to a higher category, we should look at one great advantage that this condition brings to our preaching. It represents an inescapable kinship with our hearers. In a small way, perhaps, we may look upon our earthly limitation as being to us as Jesus Christ's humanity was to him. With the Lord, of course, the taking of the form of a human and sharing even the temptations of the human was voluntary, while ours is by force of circumstances. Nonetheless, the result of keeping us on a participating level with nonclergy is that we experience the same kind of acceptance that

Christ encountered as he walked among men and women.

In fact, any assumption of being out of the realm of the earthly will be seen by the people as a sure proof of human weakness. Having observed this, a preacher has set forth this warning: ". . . exhortations delivered with any air of conscious superiority tend at once to exasperate listeners with the suspicion that the [one] who talks so confidently is taller than themselves only by the height of the pulpit."[3] And how true that last statement is —"taller . . . only by the height of the pulpit"! Our only exaltation is that we have been called to preach.

Another advantage of recognizing that our task of proclaiming the gospel has not transformed us into people immune to the evils inherent in humankind is that we develop a wholesome awareness of our own danger of falling. One preacher was so convinced that he had been placed above law that he extended this assumed immunity to the affairs of this life. He refused to keep the speed limit when driving his car; in his state a marriage license was not valid until three days after the issue, but he performed the ceremony just as soon as the document was brought to him. These and other infractions of society's rules and obligations brought him into conflict with officers of the law to whom he was only an "earthern vessel" insofar as their duty was concerned! In the area of gospel proclamation, the preacher is free to carry on ministry without compliance with Caesar. However, in other areas of life things must be given to Caesar, as taught by Jesus (Matthew 22:21). This is symbolic of the division within the preacher's being—body and spirit. The body will have its due, as will earthly rulers, and may not be ignored with safety. Try as we may to concentrate on the spiritual, the sad truth remains: "the spirit indeed is willing, but the flesh is weak" (Matthew 26:41). Our understanding of this is our salvation when we are prey to unexpected forays of temptation or despair and feel inclined to trust in an assumed immunity.

Being aware of our earthen nature does not mean that we are to flaunt our weaknesses or that we should not strive to temper all of our human contacts with the blessedness of having "been with

Jesus." Not too many years ago theological circles were toying with the thought that preachers had to "share the sin" of people if they were to be of any influence for good. One expression of this was for some clergyman to go into bars and drink with those who gathered in such places. One young preacher took a job in a distillery in his community. However, are there not at least two major reasons why this approach is not our best?

In the first place, a preacher represents to many persons a goal that seems more worthy than anything found elsewhere in life. Realizing their human weakness, these people want to have some visible example of someone with the same weakness managing to live in the presence of God. Two examples from life may point this up.

A young woman living in an apartment building found that her next-door neighbor was in such despair that she was considering suicide. The young woman arranged for her pastor to come and counsel with the troubled neighbor. When the minister came, his parishioner introduced him and added, "He is a man of God." She linked man and God, but the difference to her was that he was not only a man, but a man *of God*.

Then there was the teenaged girl whose grandmother was dying. She could not and would not accept the inevitability of death coming to one she loved so dearly. She asked her mother why their pastor, who had been making frequent calls, could not make her grandmother well. The mother replied, "But Pastor is not God." And the girl came back with, "But he is the nearest thing we've got."

The other reason why we should not put constant stress on our weaknesses is that Jesus stated our position quite clearly: "I have given them thy word; and the world has hated them because they are not of the world. . . . I do not pray that thou shouldst take them out of the world, but that thou shouldst keep them from the evil one" (John 17:14-15). Not *of* the world, but not *out* of the world. We dare not accept one of these conditions to the exclusion of the other.

Some years ago a man wrote the story of his preacher father and titled it *One Foot in Heaven*. Because of the moving of the Spirit within him at high moments of preaching, a preacher may feel that he has, albeit delicately, placed one foot tentatively in heaven. But that other foot—how solidly it is anchored on earth! This was also true of the priests of the Old Testament. At certain times they went into the holy place in the tabernacle or temple, but they always came out and took up their mundane existence in common with other people. They were never promoted to the ranks of the cherubim, seraphim, or lesser angels. Always they were human beings.

The deeper our understanding of ourselves as earthen vessels becomes, the more acute will be our desire to thwart all efforts of people to idolize us. We reminded ourselves in chapter 3 of the dismay that laid hold upon Paul when the people of Lystra considered him and his companion to be gods; he stressed the fact that "We *also* are men, of like nature with you . . ." (Acts 14:15).

We may be amused and say, "But no way would anyone in this day and age take us for gods!" But let us look at that idea. As a bus passed a certain church, two young people were heard to say, "Why, there is Dr. Jones's church!" This is all too common. Churches are designated by the name of the pastors who minister and preach there. How often do we hear sung the praises of popular radio or TV preachers! And the refrain is not "God says . . ." or "The Bible says . . ." but "Reverend So-and-So says. . . ." Each of us must have been troubled at times to hear people laud our personal qualities, *our* sermons, and so forth. All of this is much akin to the error of the people of Lystra. The tragedy of this is that the people's need and search for God are deflected and bent toward us, whose need and search for God equals theirs in every way.

So we preachers walk a fine line. We must not dwell upon our weaknesses, nor must we permit the public to forget that we have them. The endeavor is to create the true image of a preacher as a fellow pilgrim on the long, hard, upward climb to the good and holy. Like that never-to-be-forgotten pilgrim in Bunyan's book, we bear the burdens of earthly problems, cares, and failures on our backs. To make this even more vivid, we might think of a company of soldiers on a training hike; each enlisted person carries a heavy backpack and weapons, but the training officers walk without these encumbrances. As preachers we are in the ranks; we are not privileged officers. Although we lead, we share every load and discomfort of the men and women on the road.

We must not forget the reason why God chose to present his message through "earthen vessels." Perhaps there are times when we feel so inadequate to the tremendous task of being the spokesmen and women of the eternal that we question the wisdom of the arrangement. Would it not have been wiser for God either to choose unearthly beings for the mission or, if humans must be chosen, miraculously to remove our earthliness? We can find the eternal reason for God's choice in the second part of 2 Corinthians 4:7—". . . to show that the transcendent power belongs to God and not to us."

In all other endeavors men and women may train *themselves* for the profession or job at hand. Marvelous things have been done and are being done by humans. Some have gone to the moon and back. Younger people take as their examples older persons who have done much in the world. But God has reserved one thing that is utterly beyond the unassisted individual to do—preaching. We mean, of course, inspired preaching and not the poor, pallid substitutes of which we are guilty at times. True preaching is nothing more than the uncovering of the treasure that has been placed in our keeping. A sight of that treasure is all that the world needs. The sight will amaze the viewers, who will say something like the astonished people of Jesus' own country said after they had heard him speak: "Where did this man get this wisdom and these mighty works? Is not this the carpenter's son?" (Matthew 13:54*b*-55*a*). This is the kind of questioning that will turn people toward the real source of power inasmuch as they cannot believe that one of their own number—one of the human family—could possibly do what preaching requires.

This was true in the instance of the man born blind. The neighbors of the former blind man came around and looked at the man who had lived among them for many years. No longer was he groping about. He walked confidently; he looked into their eyes for the first time. In utter amazement they asked him, "How were your eyes opened?" And he told them how Jesus had given him sight. Then they inquired, "Where is he?" (John 9:8-12).

And so it will be with those of us who are the preachers. When our brothers and sisters find that we have the vision of eternal things, they will want to know how this happened to us. When we testify that the gift is from Jesus, they will want to know where he is. Is it not our dearest hope that others will see that something has happened to us, something which cannot be explained by personal effort or education, and will desperately want to find the One who has so changed us?

The "earthen vessel" concept may be illustrated further by a letter carrier. This person, who brings our mail day by day, wears the official uniform issued by authority of the government and is authorized to deliver the messages addressed to us. Among the letters in the mail person's pouch may be one of great good news. The carrier puts into our hands or mail box the letter that will fill us with joy and may change our life. But the postman did not write that letter; he or she had nothing to do with bringing into being the circumstances responsible for the good news. The letter carrier is simply the instrument used by the writer of the letter to get it to its destination. Is this not so with us as preachers? As pastors we are not part of the Good News of God's love manifested through the coming, the cross, and the resurrection of Jesus. We are the messengers wearing the livery of God's call.

Our constant awareness of our unique situation of being the custodians of the eternal Word while retaining our faulty human receptacle will send us forth to preach with greater awe than ever before, and we will never lose sight of the fact put into words by another preacher: "To preach the Word is beyond the power of sinful men, even though they are justified sinners; the Holy Spirit is the only preacher."[4]

8

Urgency

What is the mark of a true prophet—a true preacher—according to Jeremiah? It is not the preaching of peace, he said. To Hananiah, who presumed to be speaking for God and who prophesied that all would be well with Judah and that the people had nothing to fear, Jeremiah stated the matter thus: "The prophets who preceded you and me from ancient times prophesied war, famine, and pestilence against many countries and great kingdoms" (Jeremiah 28:8). And the reason why the *true* prophets found it necessary always to warn and not to encourage complacency was that they had the word of God against which to check the condition of individuals and nations.

It is as though the prophet could see the purpose and plan of God for the people as a straight track leading to pleasant pastures and still waters, always in the light of God's countenance. Being familiar with this track, the prophet saw people and nations throwing the switches of disobedience, ungodliness, and unbelief. The prophet knew that these sidetracks leading away from God's word were bound to lead to miserable situations and fatal collisions. What, then, must a faithful prophet do but cry out in urgency and plead with the errant ones to return to righteousness?

In the New Testament we find John the Baptist, Jesus, and the apostles preaching, "Repent: Turn you. Seek the straight ways."

And at what period has a preacher found the world so moral, just, and loving that no warnings were needed? If ever this time comes there will be no need for preachers.

It is certain that we, the preachers of this generation, are not in such an ideal time that we may make our preaching a pleasant addendum to all else that the world is hearing. To point this up we might consider the lesson from a chart that appeared in a news magazine in 1980. In the first column were listed those nations that had supplied themselves with nuclear weapons; the second column showed those that had advanced to the testing stage of such weapons; and the third column named the nations that were capable of producing this kind of destructive force within five years. This information alone is enough to stir a preacher to urgency in warning, but behind these statistics is the worse fact of what has impelled, and what is impelling, nations to supply themselves with a stockpile of materials that could reduce the whole world to the condition of bombed Hiroshima. What is within the hearts of men and women that brings this situation into being?

Without belittling the efforts of conferences, demonstrations, the United Nations, and antinuclear organizations, a preacher knows that logic or selfish regard for personal preservation will not change the chart or make it obsolete. Only the power of the eternal God working through repentant and obedient people can remove the fear and hatred of one another that call for "superior nuclear capability."

Indeed, there is something far more fateful than our accumulated store of bombs and warheads. The evil within us, if allowed to go unrebuked and unchecked, will lead on to a spiritual holocaust that will be explosive to a degree not possible with things made by human hands. As preachers we are working with the source of life and not primarily with the product. We remember Jesus' story of the man who was rid of the evil spirit within him and had his soul house swept and in order. For a brief moment all seemed to be well, but eight evil spirits came and occupied the emptied place and the man was worse than at the beginning (Matthew 12:43-45). How

different would have been the fate of that man if the returning evil
spirits had found the house occupied by the Spirit of God!

With the best intentions in the world, we preachers are tempted
to fight every secondary fire that we see in the lives of people and
in society while neglecting the central conflagration that is scattering
the sparks that set the many smaller fires.

The warning of the preacher's message is not like the doomful
prediction of geologists that our fossil fuel will be exhausted to a
large degree by the year 2000. Ours has the urgency of a Paul Revere
crying out, "The British are coming," meaning that the adversaries
are within sight.

Next to the urgency of the need for a warning is the urgency of
the need for rescue. There was a time when preachers thought that
the most productive thing they could do was to train and teach and
baptize the young before they fell into the evil life patterns of their
elders. But history has taught us that this laudable goal has not been
reached. The young that were under the tutelage of the preachers
of yesteryear are among those who have brought the world into its
present plight. Indeed, the young that we face today include thousands and thousands who have already joined their elders in life
patterns that are destroying them at a tender age. Prevention remains one of our great tasks, but the ministry of rescue looms large
now in the work of any preacher.

If we are to be effective in our urgency of rescue we must, by all
means, avoid the pessimism of one experienced preacher. This man
was serving on a committee to plan some joint services in his community, and the question of the program came up. Records from
several years showed that about seven hundred people could be
expected to attend. This man pointed out, "At least six hundred of
those are older people. I want a program and a place that will attract
people who are young enough to listen to a message of change.
These old people will never be any different from what they are
now. Let me see seventy vital people and I don't care about the
rest!" As inviting as this outlook appears to us at many times, it
just will not do. If rescue by God is possible and available only to

people of certain potentials and in certain age brackets, our gospel is thin indeed. Reference to the acts of Jesus will remind us that he offered his rescue to those whom we and the society of that day might class as the "unchangeables." He touched the tax-collecting bureaucrats, the professional prostitutes, the prejudiced provincials. We find that Jesus reached out to little children, mature people, and elderly leaders of the people. His message was "Whosoever will may come." Surely, if he brought his rescue to society's cast-off lepers, are we not commissioned to hold out the promise of change to moral and spiritual lepers, as well as to those who seem to us to be the desirable prospects of the kingdom?

The urgency of rescue recommends itself to us the more when we consider the condition of those who are living selfish lives apart from God. Some are still in a state of fluidity and have not, as we read in the Bible, "hardened their hearts." For them the rescue is more probable and easier. The hardened ones need a longer period in the crucible where God's love separates the dross from the gold.

This urgency, of course, must be induced in the people we are attempting to serve. Unless they can see the immediacy of their need, we can do little. Our messages always should be colored by the warning lights of these truths:

"Behold, *now* is the acceptable time; behold, *now* is the day of salvation" (2 Corinthians 6:2, author's emphasis).

". . . it is full time *now* for you to wake from sleep" (Romans 13:11*b*, author's emphasis).

". . . you do not know about tomorrow" (James 4:14).

". . . night comes, when no one can work" (John 9:4*b*).

But let us not think it will be easy to persuade people of the urgency of the need for change in their lives and in the world. We are all convinced that we have all the time in the world. People in flood areas do not heed warnings in time; people warned of hurricanes stay too long; some people in the path of the ash and lava of erupting volcanoes will not be hurried. What is true in reference to physical danger is ten- or a hundred-fold true in reference to spiritual danger. Nothing has changed in this regard since the days of the Roman governor Felix. Paul preached before him with urgency. "And as he [Paul] argued about justice and self-control and future judgment, Felix was alarmed and said, 'Go away for the present; when I have an opportunity I will summon you'" (Acts 24:25). So far as the records go, we do not find that Felix ever found it convenient to listen to more about the Lord.

We accept, of course, that we cannot expect more reaction from our hearers than we feel ourselves. If we have no sense of urgency concerning the need of all persons for God and God's power and love, then we cannot instill in others any feeling of urgency. If we believe that others are standing on solid ground but that we could direct them to something better, why hurry? But if we believe that others are in quicksand, then we do not wait until a convenient time to go to the rescue.

One preacher summed up for himself this urgency of rescue:

> When, in a burning building, I burst open a door and tell the slumbering inmate that the place is on fire, I do not balance my sentences or polish my phrases; nor does he clap his hands at the cleverness of my speech. But my solicitude and anxiety lend to my tongue an eloquence suited to the hour; and the sleeper shows his appreciation by availing himself of the opportunity of salvation.[1]

Next in order of urgency, and needing equal attention, is the urgency to help. A person pulled from quicksand may have been there so long that he or she is exhausted and in need of food and water. With a person pulled from a spiritual quagmire, tender care and the bread and water of life are needed. Someone brought out of the burning building mentioned in the previous paragraph may be suffering from smoke inhalation: in a spiritual situation the person may be suffering from sin inhalation or despair. To illustrate: A supply pastor serving a church until the arrival of the next minister was urged by the officials of the church to minister to a young man who showed signs of being open to instruction that might result in a decision to acknowledge Christ as Lord and join the church. The pastor attended to this need and, soon afterwards, baptized the lad. In his instruction the pastor had stressed the obligation of a Christian to be active in service. The convert asked that the pastor find something for him to do in the church. Since he was about to conclude his work in that parish, the pastor referred this request to the church officials and pointed out the advisability of getting the new member busy while he was so eager. Later he learned that nothing was ever done. Why should the church officials be surprised that the young man lost interest?

This matter of help is dealt with in strong terms by William James in his book *The Varieties of Religious Experience* in the chapter called "The Sick Soul." In graphic language he describes what it means to a person to be plunged into despair and melancholy until nothing in life seems right or meaningful. He concludes, "Here is the real core of the religious problem: Help! Help! No prophet can claim to bring a final message unless he says things that will have a sound of reality in the ears of victims such as these."[2] We can wonder what Mr. James would have thought of the preacher who regaled a ministers' meeting with his solution to a man's problem. The man had lost his wife; he was lonesome, without purpose, and saw his days as a dreary succession of hours to be "put in." Boastfully, the preacher told how he had persuaded this man to take dancing lessons! "He is just fine, now," said the pastor.

As preachers we can hear that desperate cry as we move among our people, as we read the news, and as statistics come across our desks totaling the number of patients in institutions for emotional disorders, the number of suicides, and the number of persons enrolled in bizarre and strange cults. The words of an old gospel song, which was used more frequently in the past than it is used today, may express this need for help: "Throw out the lifeline,/ Someone is sinking today!" Even though the imagery may seem rather archaic to us now, the point is that preachers of an earlier day had a strong conviction of the urgency of their message. They were aware of the great number of people who were sinking below the standard and the will of God for their lives, on the brink of forever failing to realize their true selves as God's beloved. Their need will not wait for a "convenient time"; it may be now or never.

Finally, we may envision the ministry with urgency as a ministry of healing. We have reviewed the matter in the terms of warning, rescuing, and helping. But, at the end, there is the same degree of urgency for healing. A person may be warned that his house is on fire; he may be pulled from the collapsing building; he may be taken to a hospital. But of what good is all this to him if he is not, then, healed?

Occasionally we will read in the newspapers or hear on the radio or see on television an urgent plea for a certain type of blood needed for a person afflicted with a particular disease. Or the cry may be for a rare antitoxin that is not regularly stocked in pharmacies or hospitals. In both cases only *one* substance will do, and that one remedy must be found or death will result.

The preacher, having reviewed the world about him and having heard the daily recital of vice, violence and viciousness of all kinds, cannot doubt that a plea is being made for the one counteracting power that can set things right. The preacher who proposes to be a factor for change in the midst of the mighty maelstrom of evil in which God's hapless children are being whirled about must know that he or she has the *one* word that can heal. As the preacher George Buttrick said, "Christian preaching in our day has that one Word from which all other words derive their life."[3] That word is of the incarnate, crucified, risen Lord—the gospel.

In brief, the message of the preacher is not one of gradualism but one of unremitting urgency. Sometimes we may be lulled by quoting from Isaiah:

> "precept upon precept, precept upon precept,
> line upon line, line upon line,
> here a little, there a little. . . ."
>
> —Isaiah 28:10

but the context tells us that this is the way the scoffers were taking the prophet's message. The prophet himself was speaking in terms of the immediate danger to those who refused to hear.

Indeed, Jesus, was not speaking of sowing seed for a sprouting in some far-off time when he said, "Do you not say, 'There are yet four months, then comes the harvest'? I tell you, lift up your eyes, and see how the fields are already white for harvest. . . . I sent you to reap . . ." (John 4:35-38). This is borne out today when we see how young people eager to find an answer to their souls' quest join themselves to cults that promise peace within.

If ever our work seems to us to take on the character of maintenance only and if we lose our recognition of emergency, it may help to remember Browning's poem "How They Brought the Good News from Ghent to Aix." A favorable turn in a war had to be reported in Aix to save that city from despair and loss, and three men started out on horseback to bear the tidings. Two fell by the wayside as their horses collapsed, but one got through. Two lines should describe to us our manner of preaching:

"I galloped, Dirck galloped, we galloped all three. . . ."
Note the word "galloped"; our ministry is not of the jogging type.

"And into the midnight we galloped abreast. . . ."
Note that "into the midnight" we gallop together—all good servants of the Lord. The night seems impenetrably black but we carry the light of the Good News to every beleaguered soul.

9

Delight in the Lord

"Man's chief end is to glorify God and enjoy him forever."[1] This statement from an old Calvinistic catechism (and one of Calvinistic roots at a time when Calvinism had the image of trending toward the somber and solemn!) catches the essence of faith. Among the facets of the true preacher, joy takes a shining place.

Often we deal with fearing God, serving God, worshiping God, trusting God, listening to God, but how often do we urge the people to emulate us in *enjoying* God? Sometimes we may be disconcerted to have a hearer say, after a sermon, "Preacher, I so enjoyed that message this morning!" As we politely murmur a word of thanks, we may be inwardly seething with the reply we would prefer to be making: "But I did not want you to *enjoy* the sermon. I wanted you to be moved and stirred until change occurred in you and you went out to change the world!" But why should we not want our hearers to rejoice in the knowledge of God's love and forgiveness and constant presence? Perhaps the one who enjoyed the message was the one of the congregation that was most adequately served by the word.

It could be questioned, too, whether or not a preacher has the ability to serve out the riches of the glories of the Eternal unless the preacher is thoroughly enjoying God. Do we not choose for our companions and friends those we enjoy being with? And have we not chosen the Lord for our lifelong companion and friend? How well the psalmist expressed this!

> In thy presence there is fulness of joy,
> in thy right hand are pleasures for evermore.
> —Psalm 16:11

Upon examination the preacher will discover that delight in the Lord is well based on his or her personal history with God and God's dealings. The past, first of all, has given abundant cause for delight in the Lord. For instance, there was the time when there was that soul-shaking and exceedingly joyful awareness that one had been led "out of darkness into his marvelous light" (1 Peter 2:9). That cataclysmic move from the dull periphery of life to the shining center has left the preacher a constantly fortified reason for joy.

At another period in life the preacher was called to a lifelong career as a witness and messenger of the gospel. No longer was there need for uncertainty as to what was the work for which he or she had been brought into the world. And every instance of preaching brought a sustaining joy of the presence of the Lord. In every fiery furnace of the world in which the preacher found opportunity for proclamation, there was that other, unseen figure who guided and preserved his servant.

And as the days and years of experience accumulated, the preacher knew the joyful realization of being abundantly fulfilled. Despite all outward oppositions and frustrations there was the inward satisfaction of one's spiritual growth and enlargement.

If ever in a low moment a preacher were to think that the joy was draining out of him or her, there need be no more than a review of the past to bring that joy surging in again at full tide.

Not only the past but the present of a preacher's life situation undergirds joy in the Lord. Is not the preacher engaged in the very center of life—"where the action is"? No matter where a preaching station is situated—whether in a remote rural area, in an inner city church surrounded by a decaying neighborhood, in a lush suburban atmosphere, or in a metropolitan spot with throngs of people—the center of life is always at the point of the preaching. As with a circuit judge who goes from city to city or town to town holding court in each, the center of the law is always at the place where the court is convened. The truth of this centering of life at the point of every proclamation of the gospel should never be surrendered. Sometimes a preacher may feel far away from the central happenings of humankind and the kingdom, and this brings discouragement. For example, when one denomination centralized its administrative activities in one magnificent new building, many pastors began to call that headquarters the "Hub." To them the most important thing in a ministerial career was to be invited to join the staff in the "Hub." They looked at all else going on among the churches as being spokes sent out from the creative center of denominational life. Nothing, of course, was further from the truth. The preacher in the smallest of the churches in that denomination was just as near, or nearer, to the center of God's work and plan as were the executives in their busy offices.

But not only are the past and present experiences of the preacher bulwarks of delight in the Lord; the future rounds out the stout bastion of joy. The future holds nothing that is not of the essence of joy. Having found how real exuberance has marked and is marking life and work, the preacher looks into the future with assurance. This is a great word expressing a great tranquillity in the face of all human events and soul storms—assurance. This was what enabled Paul to find complete contentment with all that was done to him by antagonistic people. He lived in this sure knowledge: "For me to live is Christ, and to die is gain" (Philippians 1:21).

As the preacher sums it all up, he or she—
    was called out of darkness into light,
    was assigned the task of preacher,
    was put in the way of full self-recognition,
    is set at the true center of human need,
    is assured of a future in God's presence.
How can there be less than constant delight in the Lord?

Out of all this, of course, comes the preacher's privilege of sharing and transmitting this delight to others. How is it to be done?

Perhaps the first approach will be to dispel the notion that a preacher must be, because of his or her calling and familiar involvement with the sad things of life, a doleful person. Even today we hear the expression that a preacher is a person "of the cloth," referring to the black broadcloth that was the common garb of ministers in the past. A preacher's faith should be sufficient to create a life view that will go out to the public as one of cheer and hope, despite temporal setbacks in persons and the world. If the long view is taken, dolefulness will be shown to be ridiculous in one who preaches that Jesus said, "In the world you have tribulation; but be of good cheer, I have overcome the world" (John 16:33b).

Perhaps the preacher might learn something from the approach of one doctor. His patients come to him full of concern because of certain symptoms that seem, to them, to point to serious illness or death. After this doctor makes a diagnosis that satisfies him that there is nothing radically wrong, he sends the patient away with this assurance: "*I* am not worried about it." The first reaction of the patient is "Of course, *he* is not worried about it; he is not sick. I am the one who has this thing." But after a bit of thought, the patient is much happier. "After all, the doctor does care about me. He is my friend. If he thought I had anything serious, he would be worried. If, with his knowledge and experience, he is not worried, why should I be?" Healing begins at that moment!

When people come to our preaching, they bring a myriad of problems that have them worried and fearful. They wait to hear what we have to say about their condition. They come with the question voiced in an old hymn:

> "Watchman tell us of the night,
> What its signs of promise are?"

And the preacher has the answer,

> "Traveler, darkness takes it flight;
> Doubt and terror are withdrawn."

If the preacher can give this answer with such certainty that the hearer knows that the giver utterly believes it, joyfulness is on its way.

This necessity for convincing the hearers of the preacher's unreserved acceptance of the delight to be found in serving God cannot be stressed too strongly. Here is another illustration from the medical field. A doctor had told a husband that he should persuade his wife to submit to a certain operation. The operation would make a decided change in the wife's living pattern. The distressed man inquired of the doctor, "Is this what you would insist upon your wife's doing under the same circumstances?" The doctor answered, "If I followed through on the best medical procedures, I would." That "if" exposed the doctor's limited acceptance of the value of the operation. The man went away thinking, "If this is not the best for his wife, then it is not the best for mine." So he sought the advice of another physician . The preacher cannot afford any "ifs" when speaking of God's victory over sin and death.

First, then, the preacher must be so possessed by joy in the Lord that that nonnegotiable conviction is apparent and hearers will long to have it for their own.

A second method of sharing this delight in the Lord is by tracing the golden line of joy that runs through the Bible. Cruden's concordance gives two full columns to forms of the word "joy." Tracing this on through related words, such as "delight," "cheer," "rejoice," and so forth, we find a huge reservoir of evidence available to prove that godliness is not drab, solemn, withdrawn, and uninviting.

Perhaps a good place to start is Galatians 5:19-21. After the horrible "works of the flesh" are listed, the contrasting, wholesome fruit of the Spirit follow—and the second one named is "joy"! Here, surely, joy is not thought of as a "must" that the true Christian is obliged to cultivate to prove that he or she is a true believer. On the contrary, joy, as a fruit of the Spirit, is a spontaneous thing that comes naturally to the one living by the Spirit. How could this fact have been missed by so many of the church leaders of earlier days? How could they have insisted upon the lack of color in dress or in the windows of meeting houses? How could they have repressed exuberance and any outward sign of affection among themselves? Since we are taught that joy is a gift of the Spirit, how dare we bridle it as dangerous to sound doctrine?

The hiding of joy by Christians, and especially by Christian preachers, is much like the action of a group of villagers in Africa who had received a gift from their missionary on furlough. Because of the lack of timepieces in that little settlement, the missionary had sent a sundial. When the sundial arrived, the people stood around it in admiration. It was so smooth and finished so beautifully that the new owners dreaded that something might happen to it. So they built a little hut for the sundial and put it away safe from the rays of the sun! Is not this much like the way many Christians smuggle the lovely gift of joy from the Spirit away from public view? Joy was made for public display and sharing. There is much truth in these lines by Lord Byron:

> . . . all who joy would win
> Must share it,—Happiness was born a twin.[2]

From the verses in Galatians we might turn next to Nehemiah 8:10: ". . . for the joy of the Lord is your strength." We might pause here for a moment to remember that joy has much to do with physical strength. Often we may read statements of physicians and psychologists that indicate that the person with a hopeful, joyful outlook on life has fewer ailments and emotional upsets than one with a gloomy, pessimistic outlook. This element of joy is not a physical thing; it is of the spirit of the person. What we call the "spiritual life" is tremendously heightened by joy. Joy as strength is well illustrated by the attitude of Paul and Silas in the prison at Philippi. Not only were they in prison, but they were in the inner part of the dreary building with their feet in stocks. Yet they occupied their time by singing hymns to God! (See Acts 16:25.) We are told that even Jesus was buoyed up by such strengthening joy. "Jesus . . . who for the joy that was set before him endured the cross . . ." (Hebrews 12:2).

We would not, of course, neglect the psalms that direct wor-
shipers to be in the spirit of joy. There are at least a dozen that
stress joy. What sermons could be preached on the following verses!

> . . . in thy presence there is fulness of joy.
> —Psalm 16:11
> I will offer in his tent
> sacrifices with shouts of joy
> —Psalm 27:6
> Then will I go to the altar of God,
> to God my exceeding joy.
> —Psalm 43:4
> So he led forth his people with joy,
> his chosen ones with singing.
> —Psalm 105:43

Surely the preaching and worship of today should be as per-
meated with joy as were the celebrations of old. We, as the preachers
of today, have nothing less than an obligation to keep God's people
in the spirit of joy in the Lord. P. T. Forsyth, preacher and scholar
of an earlier day, has given us this in an unforgettable expression.
He said that preaching is "the organized hallelujah of an ordered
community."[3] Preaching keeps repeating the joy that moves hearers
of the "Hallelujah Chorus." Without God this is a dismal, dis-
mayed, dying world; but (hallelujah!) the world is not without
God and is a place where goodness, hope, and love are ever to be
found. Was it not in one of the Uncle Remus books for children
that a rabbit had for himself a "laughing place"? Surely, the over-
wrought, overworked, and overworried people of any day need
for their souls, a "laughing place," and the preaching service should
be that kind of sanctuary. In a time of drought officials at the water
bureaus complain that the reservoirs are dangerously low. Is it not
entirely possible, all too possible, that many of God's children are
suffering from a drought of delight in the Lord and need a source
of renewal of their depleted reservoirs? What better place for re-
freshing than where the joyful gospel is proclaimed?

Of course, we may be accused of being Pollyannas, to whom
everything is all for the best, or of being calloused individuals who
have no feeling for the suffering in the world. We might be re-

minded of the reality of humankind's situation as worded by no less a person than Albert Schweitzer: "Only at quite rare moments have I felt glad to be alive. I could not but feel with a sympathy full of regret all the pain that I saw around me, not only that of men, but of the whole creation."[4] But delight in the Lord and constant compassion and understanding are not contrasting emotions.

Our joy in the Lord is based on eternal and never-failing hope. Of course we feel all the woes of people as they make their pilgrimage through this world. But we know that there is a loving God who is our sustaining power through all that may happen to us here and who points us to a glorious fulfillment out of our struggles. Our kind of joy, that which we preach, is not the effervescent feeling that comes from physical or emotional comfort and ease but is a deep-seated life-force that cannot be quenched by conditions or things. If we need a living illustration of this, we may refer again to Paul. Few people, if any, have equaled his sharing of suffering of body and mind; few, if any, have been as concerned with the plight of others. And yet, as we have mentioned before, Paul always came out of his experiences "rejoicing." Having found the joy of the Lord on the road to Damascus, Paul went through the world with assurance: ". . . I have learned, in whatever state I am, to be content. I know how to be abased, and I know how to abound; in any and all circumstances I have learned the secret of facing plenty and hunger, abundance and want. I can do all things in him who strengthens me" (Philippians 4:11-13). Paul knew that his life was a mission, a mission that brought him nearer to his Lord as each moment came and passed. This was his joy and this brought him the inner contentment that nothing could disturb. This is the joy that we preach. In exultation we proclaim:

> The earth is the LORD's and the fulness thereof,
> the world and those who dwell therein. . . .
> —Psalm 24:1

The preacher has something working already as he or she gives the ringing message that godly people cannot but have fullness of joy. Joy may already have entered the hearts of some who cannot quite tell its source. Dostoevsky, the Russian writer, noticed that "the joyful can never be godless."[5] And C. S. Lewis expressed the coming of faith to him as "Surprised by Joy," the title he gave to his autobiography.

10

Social Consciousness

Two words were sufficient to cause divisions in many churches—even in denominations—a few decades ago. The words were "social gospel." The factions of congregations split by this supposedly new concept gathered around one of two standards:

"Let the church be the church."

"Let the church be relevant to the material needs of humankind."

As the years have passed, there has been a wholesome effort to reconcile the two approaches. Is not the church being itself when it ministers to the whole person? Is there not relevancy when the church interprets the life that is supported by ministering to physical needs? Even so, the problem has not been completely solved and continues to perplex preachers. To what extent, if any, should sermons be devoted to pronouncements on current events, political items, war, oppression, and so forth?

"Social gospel" is not mentioned often now, except in extreme circles, and has been superceded by the term "involvement." The church is called upon to be part and parcel of all that is happening in the world. This was especially true in the sixties. After the assassination of President Kennedy, large groups of Christians gathered to confess their share in the sin of the killing. Preachers were among the demonstrators in civil rights marches and other protests. There was much pounding of the pulpit against the war in Vietnam. Priests and other ministers were arrested for sharing in the burning of draft cards. One church, known to the author, mortgaged its property and purchased several housing units for low-income people. Minority people were deliberately and selectively elected to the highest offices in councils of churches and denominations. Rules were passed that no clergy placement committee was to mention the race of any candidate being recommended to a church.

During this frenzy of involvement a certain man was transferred to a job in a strange city. Before deciding upon a church to which to transfer his membership, he went from church to church to see what each was saying. After the service in one of these churches, he spoke to the minister and said, "I was refreshed this morning. You did not beat me over the head to get out there and do something about war and racial injustice and poverty. During the week I do get out there and do whatever I can. But how can the churches expect people like me to go on day after day expending spiritual energy without replenishing our souls at the source once a week?"

In all of this introduction, the preacher may begin to recognize his or her own personal struggle. The preacher wants to serve God and serve the present generation, but what is the best way to do it? Even the New Testament supplies ammunition for both sides of the struggle. Jesus, speaking of the anxiety to have the essentials of life—food, drink, clothing—said, "But seek first his kingdom and his righteousness, and all these things shall be yours as well" (Matthew 6:33). And yet, in the chapter on the great judgment (Matthew 25), he condemns those who failed to relieve the physical needs of the "least of these my brethren." Going on, we find that when a woman poured expensive ointment on his feet and a disciple protested that the ointment should have been sold and the money acquired used to feed the poor, he said, "You always have the poor with you, and whenever you will, you can do good to them; but you will not always have me" (Mark 14:7). And then we come to the place where multitudes had followed him without having made provisions for food. Jesus said to the disciples, ". . . you give them something to eat" (Matthew 14:16).

We could add many illustrations, but we find that Jesus, while never without concern for the needs of the body, stressed the "one thing needful." Perhaps we might better understand the main teaching through this statement:

> ". . . you tithe mint and dill and cummin, and have neglected the weightier matters of the law, justice and mercy and faith; these you ought to have done, without neglecting the others. . . . first cleanse the inside of the cup and of the plate, that the outside also may be clean" (Matthew 23:23, 26).

Is not the preacher's divine mission to put stress on the weightier matters and to strive to cleanse the inside of the person first? Perhaps some analogies may help.

The teachers in the Army, Navy, and Air Force academies are not regularly directing the outcome of military operations; they are training young people who will go out and direct military operations. The instructors in medical colleges are not often found in positions of chief-of-staff in hospitals or leading research teams seeking cures for diseases; they are training the people who will do these things. Also, the instructors in law schools are not chiefly engaged in arguing cases in courts or serving in legislatures; they are training new lawyers who will be skilled to dispense and secure justice under all circumstances. If these teachers were forever deserting their task of preparing future professionals and insisting on going hither and thither at every indistinct trumpet call, where and how would the world find trained physicians, lawyers, and people for defense? And is it not so with the preacher? Who is to be used by the Spirit to bring men and women, boys and girls into a redemptive relationship with God, which will cleanse the source of their being until they will be the champions in the world of all that is true and good and just and lovely and of good report? Who will do this if not the preacher? The preacher is to respond by personal participation only on a strict, selective basis.

Two points of view may be examined as to the best procedure

for combatting all that is wrong. Thoreau has this to offer: "There are a thousand hacking at the branches of evil to one who is striking at the root. . . ."[1] And a denominational director of evangelism advanced this idea: "We must strike at the 'structures' of society. We are not saved individually but in our relationships to all others." We see truth in both approaches, but we might say that all "structures" are made up of individuals. It takes quite a bit of leaven to raise the "whole lump."

The crucial decision for the preacher to make is at what angle sin and wrong and injustice are to be attacked. If the preacher is the only one called to be a maker of wholesome leaven, his or her chief occupation seems to be to make the leaven in preference to banging headforemost into every sorry and sordid "lump" in the world. However, we must agree that each preacher is obliged to follow what path the Lord lays open in each situation.

Wistfully, at times, every preacher longs for the realization of the prophecy in Micah:

> . . . nation shall not lift sword against nation,
>   neither shall they learn war any more;
> but they shall sit every man under his vine and under his fig tree,
>   and none shall make them afraid.
>
> —Micah 4:3-4

In this description of the ideal situation for all people we find:
   the end of all war;
   the undisputed right of everyone to what is his or her own;
   a place for everyone;
   freedom of the individual;
   ample food supply for all;
   freedom from fear of violence or usurpation.
In these few words the prophet has summed up that for which we yearn most earnestly. If only the world of our day could be that kind of world!

Well then, we might say to ourselves as preachers, if that is our ideal why not give all time and effort to bringing the prophecy to an actuality? For a preacher there is one catch there. Suppose that we, working mightily with others of like mind and spirit, could remake our world into that fashion, is there nothing more to be desired? And in response there will come to us the statement of Jesus: "For what will it profit a man, if he gains the whole world and forfeits his life?" (Matthew 16:26). If the people under their *own* vines and fig trees are not changed persons, if they have not experienced the new birth by the Spirit, if this life is all that they know, then there is no inner peace or joy. How long, could we suppose, would our ideal situation continue? How long would it be before war would be revived, how long before crime and violence would emerge again, how long before strutting militarists and dictators would again cause poverty and oppression? With all the good things foretold by Micah, there must be included what an advertiser called the "priceless ingredient." Without God, this beautiful world with all that it has to offer, the companionship of our fellows, and the good things for the mind and body have no savor. Without God, all is flat. Knowing this, the preacher will take a fresh look at the glory and immensity of the message entrusted to God's apostles.

Two illustrations may help here. The first is a fable from an old philosophical work.

In the seventeenth century, three peasants were walking along a country road. To their amazement, they came to a man lying in the road. They observed this person carefully. His flesh was well-rounded and had a good color, and the man showed every evidence of having been well fed. His clothes were of fine quality and sufficient for the season. His skin was such that they knew he must have been accustomed to shelter from the weather. His face was that of an intelligent person; he must have been privileged in things of the mind. So the three peasants decided that there was nothing wrong with the one lying athwart their path. He had had food, clothing, shelter, and the good things of the world. So why did he not get up and go his way? Carefully, they set the body on its feet and balanced it. But when they let go, the body fell to earth again. Three times they stood the body up on its feet, and three times it dropped. In bewilderment the three travelers went their way, saying among themselves, "There is just nothing wrong with that man. Everything about him is all right, but he won't stand up." The one thing that the man lacked, of course, was life. He had had everything that the peasants considered necessary and desirable in the world, but all of these advantages did him no good without life. Jesus did not say that he had come that all might have material, earthly possessions, or freedom from molestation. What he said was, "I came that they may have life, and have it abundantly" (John 10:10). The other illustration is, I think, original with me.

Let us think of two stores dealing in medicines. The first is the old-fashioned pharmacy. Nothing is sold there but prescribed drugs and other healing agents. The other store is a modern drugstore that offers a wide variety of merchandise in addition to medicines. In fact, it is more like a small department store than a true drugstore. The owner displays wares found in specialty shops such as hardware stores, novelty stores, confectioneries, stationery stores, and small appliance stores.

Into this drugstore comes a man with a prescription from his doctor. The physician has told this man that it is urgent that he have the medicine if he is to live. He relates this to the druggist, but suppose the druggist smiles and leads him to the health food section. He says, "What you need is nourishment for that great body of yours," and he sells him some food. In a day or two the man is back to say that he is no better. Then suppose the druggist takes him to the sporting goods aisle and says, "What you need is this warm jacket to protect you from the cold outside," and he sells him the garment. A third time the man comes in with the prescription in his hand and wants the medicine. This time suppose the druggist leads him to the appliance department and sells him a TV. "What you really need," he says, "is a new mental outlook." Wearily the man walks home, wondering to himself, "That is the only store that has medicine. I could have bought these other things from other stores. These are good things, but I need the medicine."

The man never returns to the drugstore because he dies.

The preacher has life to offer; the preacher has life-sustaining truth. The preacher has his or her own specialty that no other can provide.

Now, with the thought-stage set, what definite things can the preacher do that will move toward achieving the composite goal of helping everyone—

to know God, from the least to the greatest, and

to sit unhindered under one's own "vine and fig tree,"
fearing no evil?

The prophets have much to teach us and can guide us in our search for the proper way to respond to the social needs of people.

Amos, in his pronouncements against the wrongs being perpetrated in his time, always starts off with "Thus says the LORD. . . ." We find this authoritative word preceding these phrases:

> they sell the righteous for silver,
>   and the needy for a pair of shoes—
> they trample the head of the poor into the dust of the earth
>   and turn aside the way of the afflicted;
> a man and his father go in to the same maiden, . . .
>   upon garments taken in pledge. . . .
>
> —Amos 6:6-8

Amos shows us that all that is good in the world is the result of obedience to the law of God, and all that is wrong in the world is because of disobedience to the law of God. The prophet, the preacher, is to be moved in utterance not simply by humanitarian, ethical, or enlightened motives but by the knowledge of the will of God for persons and nations. For generations, the world has had a plethora of sociologists, philosophers, teachers, "do-gooders," pacifists, economists, and the like, but—as has been noted earlier in this book—the world is not improving. We preachers may speak and serve in the unique way of bringing God's word to bear against the problems.

Micah went at the conditions existing in the world in the same mood, saying,

> and what does the LORD require of you
> but to do justice, and to love kindness,
> and to walk humbly with your God?
> —Micah 6:8

Using these three requirements, Micah could build his sermons to touch all of the relationships of person to person. These requirements of God have never changed, and today's preachers may use them without reservations.

Hosea announced,

> ". . . for it is the time to seek the LORD. . . .
> You have plowed iniquity,
>   you have reaped injustice,
>   you have eaten the fruit of lies.
> . . . you have trusted in your chariots
>   and in the multitude of your warriors. . . .
> —Hosea 10:12-13

Joined here with the list of wrongs is the evangelistic thrust: "seek the LORD." In Hosea's list of evils we find many thoughts that are relevant to our time. For instance, the Israelites trusting in chariots and warriors is very much like nations today counting their tanks and aircraft, depending upon the balance of power and nuclear deterrents.

A thorough search of the utterances of the prophets, major and minor, will reinforce the illustrations cited. We do not preach Utopia or a new Atlantis; we preach the kingdom of God.

For a modern example of what may be done, we Christians—Protestants and Catholics alike—may observe the method of Pope John Paul II when he visited the United States. In the course of his travels he said many pertinent and true things concerning the need for change in many areas of personal, national, and international life. But at the center of his message was the Mass—the celebration of what Jesus did on the cross. We might learn much by remembering that there were far greater crowds to participate in the observance of Christ's sacrifice than there were to hear the pope's sermonettes. This may say something as to the deepest need of men and women.

P. T. Forsyth, theologian of an earlier generation, stresses the need for preachers to be consumed by a sense of the holiness of God. He teaches that it was the holiness of God that was demonstrated at the cross, and that it is God's holiness that must be the basis of our approach to the world. He said to preachers: "Our great positive task, therefore, is not social reform, political pressure, or philanthropic energy, but something which empowers and fertilizes all of these."[2]

We have a wide world to face, to serve, and to change. Our message is sufficient for the whole person and all of the needs that are felt.

11

Craftsmanship

The number 52 is a sobering, if not appalling, number for preachers: 52 Sundays calling for sermons! Even if 4 may be deducted for vacation and perhaps 4 more for special occasions or guest speakers, the remaining 44 stretch out ominously through the church year. The unremitting regularity of the demand, Sunday after Sunday, for the preacher's message from God can affect a person in one of two ways.

If a preacher has disorganized methods of sermon·making, the long road of pulpit appearances could well be frightening and depressing. However, if he or she puts forth smoothly disciplined efforts, the preaching schedule can well be challenging, joyful, and blessed.

This chapter will endeavor to point out ways of preparing sermons that can be of help as the preacher works toward a personal routine that is best for him or her.

Selecting the Subject or Topic

The topic or subject of the sermon names the goal toward which all of the preparation leads. Before any sermon can be brought together intelligently and cohesively, the preacher must know the end result desired. Leacock, a writer of humor, told of a man who "mounted his horse and rode off in all directions." Many sermons of this kind have been preached, and hearers will go away saying to one another, "I don't know what that sermon was all about, do you?" This is tragic because twenty-five minutes a week is a very short period for the public proclamation of the Word. First, then, let us examine sources from which sermon subjects are drawn.

A preacher will find his themes by inspiration of the Spirit, study, and—as Virgilius Ferm has said—by keeping "an ear to the pavement."[1] Some sources from which topics come are:

Prayer

Meditation

Reading: the Bible, books, magazines, newspapers, advertisements

Study: any and all subjects that have to do with God and humankind

The church calendar year: this lectionary may be found in service books of the Episcopal, Lutheran, Presbyterian, Catholic churches and a few other denominations

Church holy days: Christmas, Easter, Pentecost, etc.

National holidays: Thanksgiving, New Year's Day, etc.

Observation: people in various situations, nature, TV presentations—particularly the news and documentaries

Events: current local and world happenings

Counseling: in crises of life—marriage, bereavement, career choices, family problems, emotional upsets, guilt trauma

Visitations in the homes of members and others

Assessment of the preacher's own inner drives and needs

With these varied and rich sources always available, the preacher should have no difficulty in coming upon themes vital to the life of the congregation. Frequently what comes may be the subject for more than a single sermon. A great concern may require several sermons to develop properly.

Deciding upon the Type of Sermon

After the preacher has decided upon the subject, he or she determines the category into which it will fall. The four general types are:

Doctrinal: These include such subjects as faith, grace, redemption, eternal life, the church, sin, and so forth.

Expository: A block of Scripture may be found that fits the theme and may be opened up to the congregation.

Textual: A verse or two may be sufficient in richness to satisfy the needs of the sermon.

Topical: The subject may be one that requires a search of the Bible for the teachings that relate to it.

The direction of the preparation will be guided by the type and form of the sermon. For the doctrinal type, books of respected theologians will be needed; for the expository and textual types, Bible studies, commentaries, and various versions of the Bible will be helpful; for the topical type, a concordance and secular works that deal with the theme will be required. In all instances the latest books in each field should be consulted as well as the tried and true. Nothing will dull a sermon more than to bring it out of a musty past of scholarship for presentation to people of the closing years of the twentieth century.

The Outline

Now we are ready to determine an outline. Only rare preachers have the ability to sit down and write a sermon without an outline. Such gifted persons may skip this section! The others of us, however, sorely need an outline as a guide to save us from lack of direction and wandering. An outline may be constructed as follows:

Introduction

An arresting statement or illustration may be used to inform the congregation of the purpose and aim of the sermon (it is well to write the introduction last of all—after the main body of the message has been completed; then the preacher will know exactly what is to be introduced).

At this point it may be well to look at a rubric popular in writers' conferences:

HEY! YOU! SEE! SO.

In a sermon the introduction is both the "Hey!" and the "You!" If the preacher is to secure and keep attention during the preaching, the hearers must be captured (Hey!) and must be convinced that what they are about to hear vitally concerns each one of them (You!).

Two examples of sermon introductions may be helpful.

The first is one that was used by a pastor on the first Sunday he preached in a new parish.

> If I were you sitting there in a pew this morning, and if I had taken part in selecting a new pastor for my church, and if I knew that much of the money I contribute to the church (often at the sacrifice of desirable things) would go toward that preacher's support and the rest of it to causes approved by that person, and if I were aware that my religious thought would be colored by that pastor, and if I realized that our young people might find in this leader either a worthy example of Christian living or one that would bring them to a tragic disbelief in the holiness of life, and if I knew that my own home might be made stronger under this ministry or weaker to the point of breaking—well, I would ask the speaker standing in the pulpit (and I would have every right to ask), "Preacher, what have you to say for yourself?"
> That is a question which I feel obliged to answer now.

The second introduction was used for a sermon titled "The Innocent Bystander in Life." The text was John 9:3—"Jesus answered, 'It was not that this man sinned, or his parents, but that the works of God might be made manifest in him.'" The sermon introduction was as follows:

> Do you know the name of the blind man in the morning lesson? No, neither do I, nor does anyone else. And I think there is a good reason for this—perhaps he is forever nameless in order that you, and I, might give our names in turn to this person who was a typical "bystander" in life. And how often do you and I occupy that position! How often do we have things happen to us over which we have no control and for which we are not responsible! Suddenly, and without warning, life hits us a staggering blow with no apparent reason or purpose.
> This morning we ask ourselves, we ask God, "Why?"

Notice the "Hey!" and the "You!" in both of the illustrations.

Main Points

A sermon may have an indefinite number of main points. The character of the sermon and its manner of presentation will determine whether one or several divisions will be needed. The main points are the "See!" of the rubric—the working out of the thesis or exhortation at hand. A variation in this part of the sermon is advisable since the hearers, after months of listening to the same preacher, may class him or her as "a three-pointer" or "six-pointer" and try to follow the development in order to estimate how much longer the sermon will last! If there is to be more than one point, the preacher should be careful to see that each one works into the next in order to build to a logical and growing climax. One professor advised his students to use a three-point sermon in this way: "Start low, go higher, take fire!" Each point should have more appeal and urgency than the one preceding or there is apt to be a monotony which will kill the attention of the congregation.

For instance, let us suppose that the sermon is on John 3:16. A monotonous way of working out the text might be:

    I. God's Love
    II. The Object of God's Love
    III. The Method of God's Love
    IV. The Result of God's Love

A more dynamic division might be:

    I. God Has a Passionate Love for the World
    II. God's Love Demanded God's Most Costly Gift
    III. God's Love in Sacrifice Brings Us Life Eternal

The main points, as the "See!" of the rubric, must make good on the promise of the introduction, or the sermon does not keep faith with the hearers.

Subpoints

If the preacher finds various facets of the main point that deserve titles of their own, then it is well to so divide the presentation. Also, a subpoint is helpful for the preacher's memorization of the material.

Taking one of the main points mentioned, it might be worked out in this way:

    I. God Has a Passionate Love for the World
        A. The intensity of that love ("so loved")

B. The world as the object of that love

Here again it must be noted that, as with the main points, subpoints are used only as required and never manufactured in order to keep within a set pattern. Nothing is more deadly for a preacher or the congregation than for the sermons to fall neatly into the same order week after week. A seminary assistant pointed this out to the senior minister of the church: "If the people like the type of sermon you preach, they can be absolutely sure of getting it every Sunday." If this was intended as a compliment, it was certainly of the left-handed variety!

The Conclusion

The conclusion is the "So" of the rubric. If the preacher has been successful in the introduction—gaining attention, showing that the sermon subject vitally concerns each of the hearers, and telling what question or problem of life will be dealt with—and if in the main body of the sermon the preacher has dealt effectively with that problem or question, then the conclusion exhorts the hearers to do something about what has been presented. One well-known preacher related that when he was new at the task, he preached a most eloquent and moving sermon on some community need and felt a glow of pride when he had finished. But before he could announce the closing hymn, someone in the rear of the church, who was mightily convinced by the sermon, rose up and asked, "Just what did you have in mind for us to do, Dominie?" The preacher was embarrassed and devastated because he had not given thought to—had not expected to suggest—action. His sermon had no conclusion—no "So," no "therefore. . . ."

Some New Testament conclusions to sermons are worth reviewing. After Peter's sermon on Pentecost the question was asked, "'Brethren, what shall we do?' And Peter said to them, 'Repent, and be baptized every one of you in the name of Jesus Christ . . .'" (Acts 2:37-38). After one of Paul's exhortations he used this conclusion: "I appeal to you therefore, brethren, by the mercies of God, to present your bodies as a living sacrifice, holy and acceptable to God, which is your spiritual worship" (Romans 12:1). And

Jesus, having preached on unforgiveness and the punishment of the merciless, said, "So also my heavenly Father will do to every one of you, if you do not forgive your brother from your heart" (Matthew 18:35). Without a definite and challenging conclusion, a sermon may be more or less a waste of time.

Illustrations

Illustrations or the lack of them can make or break a sermon. Illustrations may be thought of as breaths of fresh air to ventilate the depth and profundity that must be part of sermons dealing with eternal things, as windows to throw light across serious considerations, or as translators to put theological truths into the experience of today's people.

But the illustrations to be used must be carefully selected. They are never to be thought of as "stories" to break the sermon into digestible portions; such illustrations cut the continuity of the presentation and the preacher will not be able to bring his or her congregation back to the main line. In the earlier chapters of this book the author has tried to demonstrate the helpfulness of illustrations that fit the subject under discussion.

Where are illustrations to be found? The sources of sermon subjects listed at the beginning of this chapter may, for the most part, be fruitful for the finding of illustrations, also. Congregational reaction proves that the most popular and acceptable illustrations are those from real life. The life of the preacher, as the years go on, will provide many telling illustrations that may be used without affectation. From the lives of people the preacher meets day by day will come useful stories. Literature may be tapped, but with care. A narrative or anecdote from a book may be used, but beware of long quotations!

If one criterion should be used above others in the selection of the illustrations, it would be that of familiarity. If the hearers cannot identify with the illustration, no good has been done.

By all means, a preacher should build up a personal file of illustrations. Books of illustrations may be purchased, but this "canned" variety rarely has any vitality.

To indicate how a congregation reacts to a "down-to-earth" illustration, this incident may be revealing. A preacher had a point about indecision in the sermon; to illustrate, he told a story about how he and his wife had gone to a store to buy a new refrigerator. They saw two that were within their price range and that were adequate for their needs. After due consideration they made a choice. Then they went home to await delivery. "And," said the preacher, "after we got home and reviewed the merits of the two refrigerators, what do you suppose we said to each other?" A voice from the audience answered the question: "You wished you had bought the other one!" The congregation laughed because this was an experience common to all; which of them had not gone through the same agony of indecision? From that moment the congregation listened in rapt attention until the sermon ended. The preacher was one of them!

Humor

Is humor ever acceptable in a sermon? By all means, if it is in good taste and relevant. All of us are tempted to repeat a good joke that will loosen up the congregation, but jokes, as such, have no part in preaching. Preachers should use a light touch in humor. Amusing situations from real life are much to be preferred over humorous tidbits from books or the like. A touch of humor for each main point is not excessive. We must never "drag in a story by the hair of the head" so that people will say later, "That was funny, but what did it have to do with the sermon?"

Jesus should be our example in the use of illustrations and humor. As we read his sayings, especially the parables, are we not able to understand the deep truths by means of the pictures and extravagances of speech that enrich the preachments?

Before we close the discussion on humor, we might do well to listen to a Victorian poet and keep fresh in our memory what he said about preachers he had heard:

> 'Tis pitiful
> To court a grin, when you should woo a soul;

To break a jest, when pity would inspire
Pathetic exhortation; and to address
The skittish fancy with facetious tales
When sent with God's commission to the heart.[2]

It is a strait and narrow path we walk as preachers when it comes to humor.

Is the sermon now ready to deliver? Not quite. One preacher said that he prepared his sermons from Monday to Friday and prepared the preacher on Saturday. He was heeding what an earlier preacher had learned: "The man and the message are one." Much prayer and meditation go into the sermon if it is to be fit to pronounce before a gathering of God's children.

When the sermon is being preached, the eloquence and diction and energy of the preacher cannot change lives except that the Spirit is moving. We know this, and that is why Monday morning is often a bleak time as we remember the sermon in its imperfection.

12

Expectations

A preacher had a dream. . . .

In this dream the preacher came to a zoo. There he saw the caged animals and birds. Their confinement prevented their using their God-given abilities and potential. The birds had wings but were not free to soar loftily at great distances. The animals had legs for running but could only pace wearily around a constricted area. All had gregarious instincts for seeking out others of their kind and establishing families and communities. All had a purpose from the Creator to preserve the balance of nature and, thus, to be a blessing to humankind.

The preacher was grieved by what he saw and what he could imagine of the hopeless and monotonous existence of the poor creatures. Then, in the dream, the preacher saw that the walking-stick he held in his hand had become a magic wand. Quickly, he opened door after door until every one of the prisoners was free. With ecstatic happiness he watched the animals and birds return to their rightful homes in the wilderness.

When the preacher awakened, he realized that he would soon be in the pulpit. Still wondering about the sermon he was to preach, he remembered the dream. Then he knew its meaning. Before him were people, each of whom was caged to some degree by sin, sorrow, helplessness or despair. It came to him that he was in a pulpit because God had given him the magic wand with which to release these men, women, boys, and girls and set them free to use all of their talents, love, faith and service to the fullest.[1]

This dream and its meaning embody the secret to our understanding of the results of preaching. As the cages are opened and the people go out from a preaching service, things happen that could never have happened except for the freedom given by the Spirit of God working through the preacher.

The fundamental thing that happens is that lives are changed. These people are no longer confined but are like the person in Masefield's "The Everlasting Mercy":

> The bolted door had broken in,
> I knew that I had done with sin.
> I knew that Christ had given me birth
> To brother all the souls on earth. . . .[2]

These people go out and soon have shaken off the dust and dampness of whatever prison had held them. They clear their lungs of the fetidness of limited living in mean circumstances and seize upon their inheritance as the sons and daughters of God. Paul, in his prison in Rome, must have remembered his spiritual jail, which had held him until the door was opened on his way to Damascus, because he wrote of the freedom that was his in Christ Jesus. The liberated person no longer runs in place but runs free to do the will of the Almighty.

Preaching starts great movements in the world. We do not need to think of world-shaking, headlining endeavors but of the efforts that grow out of our own preaching. We see our hearers engaged in feeding the hungry (in movements such as senior citizens' dinners and meals-on-wheels), in tutoring underprivileged children, in preparing packages of cheer to be taken to prisons, in sewing garments for the world relief movement, in chauffering disabled persons to doctors, in spreading the gospel by teaching church school classes and by exemplifying the Christian attitude toward life, in spotting community ills and needs that require concerted action, in becoming a part of the world missions movement through contributions and promotions, in discharging the duties of good citizens conscientiously, and in being part of many national and international efforts toward peace and world fellowship. Oh, it would be grand to be in the company of the London preacher heard by Wilfred Grenfell, who was moved to give himself to the secluded people of Labrador as a medical missionary, and in the company of the speaker at Aldersgate heard by John Wesley, whose heart was "strangely warmed" and who went forth to begin what came to be the Methodist movement. But are we not in their company? In addition to the many individual changes and efforts we have listed, is there not the eminent possibility that some people in our many audiences will be the instigators of tremendous things? And that none of our hearers who find freedom will rush out of the open cage without movement in the right direction?

Preaching enlarges and strengthens the church. However, "the church" is more than the group to which we preach. If our preaching resulted in someone uniting with some other local congregation, we have enlarged and strengthened the church. When Billy Graham, or some other evangelist, has preached and a number of persons come forward to indicate their decision to become part of the body of Christ, they do not go to one church but scatter out into many churches. However, we must agree that the preaching has enlarged the church. A preacher should never be downcast by the statistics showing the number of people that have been added to his or her particular church since it cannot be known how many go from the preaching and eventually become active members of some other gathered body of Christians.

The strengthening comes from the addition of each new person and from the renewed energy, insight, and devotion to the work that Christ left for the church body to do in the world. In light of all that the world needs from the church today, we can say at any time, "The harvest is plentiful, but the laborers are few" (Matthew 9:37). As it was from Peter's sermon on Pentecost, so it is with our preaching—that those who are convicted are "added" to the church.

Preaching is a strong bulwark against godlessness and falsity. There has always been a strong tide of unbelief and untruth eroding the shore of godliness and truth, and it seems that in our time this tide has increased in height and violence until we are appalled to observe the inroads being made on once solid areas of life. It is a rare newscast that does not start off with a list of the crimes committed during the past twelve hours. The headlines in the newspapers are quite uniformly given to captions of stories about the latest horrible things that have occurred in the nation and world. Here we might pause to question what preaching can do about all of this. Is not preaching only talk? Do not the gang lords, the drug pushers, the sexual hedonists, the warmongers, and the self-indulgent laugh at us for being impotent crybabies? If they do take us lightly, they do not know history. Were not Jesus' teachings "talk"? And were not Paul's preachings and Savonarola's pronouncements and John Calvin's exhortations and Martin Luther's thunderings and John Wesley's sermons just "words"? Ah, but all of these were talk with a difference. True, preaching is made up of words, but the preacher, as no other talker, has been commissioned by God to go out and say to the people: "Thus saith the Lord!"

It is this divine ingredient in our preaching that gives us confidence that we are having results in our resistance to evil. We are not using a broom of words, as King Canute used a broom to sweep back the sea; we are using the building stones of God's commandments and purpose to set up dykes to frustrate wickedness. Indeed, the preaching will not only conserve what godliness there is in the world but will reclaim lost territory by the power of the Spirit.

Another result of preaching is the nurturing of holiness in the world. It is a temptation to take the Isaiah attitude toward holiness:

> "Holy, holy, holy is the LORD of hosts. . . .
> . . . I am a man of unclean lips. . . ."
> —Isaiah 6:3, 5

In other words, God is holy; we are not. But are we permitted to live by this limited assessment of holiness? Let us remember that

". . . he disciplines us for our good, that we may share his holiness" (Hebrews 12:10*b*). There is a uniformity of teachings in both Testaments that all should strive toward holiness in order to have kinship with God. Holiness and cleanliness are related. When the early Hebrews were to come before God in worship, they were told to be sure they were holy—clean. But it is inner cleanliness that we are dealing with today. Jesus pointed out that environment—what goes into people—is not the important thing; what comes out of people—words, thoughts, actions—is what matters.

If we could we could think of our preaching as the burning coal from the altar of God that once purified the unclean lips of Isaiah and can cleanse lives today, we would be awe-stricken in the knowledge of the character of our task. Perhaps we could agree with James Robinson as he summed up the preacher's charge: "A preacher is more than a writer of sermons and a pastor of a congregation; he is the rung of a ladder from man to God. . . ."[3] And we may be sure that the nurturing of holiness in persons is the prime requisite in starting them on the climb toward God.

Another and perhaps less obvious result of preaching is the placing in proper perspective of the permanent and temporary in life.

If we need a good illustration of the permanent and the temporary, we may find it in the parable of the prodigal son. The permanent is represented by the father's love, the father's house where the son had an assured place, the inheritance of things that belonged to the father. The temporary is all that is gathered up in the two words "loose living." Loose living must have meant in that day what it means now: unwise and wasteful use of the body, the squandering of what the father gives, purposelessness and lack of any contribution to the world or to the needs of others, and association with the immoral and the sharing of their dissipation.

Perhaps this description of the temporary may seem extreme, but it is fairly complete so that anyone may find something in it that strikes home in a personal way. The issue comes down to a matter of values. We understand by the parable that the son had to choose between living with his father in his father's house and loose living. The two situations could never be compatible. Thus, anything that can be done in the sight of God has in it something of the permanent, and anything that must be done apart from God is surely temporary.

Another way to get at the nature of the temporary and the permanent is to examine the thirteenth chapter of First Corinthians. The temporary things are listed as those consigned to "passing away." The permanent things (faith, hope, love) are those that will "abide."

Preaching can help persons to devise tests for themselves that will help them put the temporary and permanent under scrutiny. For instance, when the Super Bowl football game was played in 1981, many people spent several thousand dollars and three days of life in order to see that sport contest. Put to the test, these persons would need to ask themselves, "Did I use my money to the best advantage? Was it wise to give that much of my life (which can never be recovered) just to watch a game? Was that the most important thing I could have done with my treasure and my time?" This is not to be puritanical and say that recreation is wrong, but it is to point up the issues of "first" things in life. Preaching should not be judgmental or investigative of anyone's life routine, but it does have an obligation to help hearers analyze the offerings of life and to help them develop an ability to sort out the temporary from the permanent. The ancient Greek writer Heraclitus came to this conclusion: "Donkeys would choose garbage rather than gold."[4] Preaching makes the distinction between garbage and gold.

Going further, we can say that preaching results in displaying the kingdom of God. It refutes the idea that God has given up on the world and that we are to find the kingdom only in the "Sweet By and By." Preachers can truly preach that each redeemed person is part of God's kingdom, and since redeemed persons are to be found in unnumbered spots in this world, it follows that the kingdom is among us. Just as we find citizens of our country in far-off places and find in many countries "English colonies," "American sectors," "German neighborhoods," "Italian streets," and so forth, so do the citizens of God's kingdom take that kingdom wherever they go. Each one is an outpost of the kingdom.

Wherever we find the qualities that Jesus taught as characteristic of his kingdom, we find that kingdom. Wherever there is compassion, unselfish love, the search for truth, reverence for life, sacrifice of personal gains for the good of the whole—there is the kingdom. Of course, some humanists, cultists, and quasi-communists may try to appropriate these things of the kingdom and credit them to the impulses of men and women apart from God, but preaching can point out the errors and hold up that which composes the "fruit of the Spirit." Of these who claim as their own the kingdom's assets, the preaching says, as Joshua said to Israel: "Thus says the LORD. . . . it was not by your sword or by your bow. I gave you a land on which you had not labored . . ." (Joshua 24:2,12-13). Just as the American embassy in a foreign country may employ people of the country to do work that furthers the mission of the embassy and these workers are not citizens of the United States, so we shall see many engaged in kingdom work who are not of the kingdom. But that does not invalidate the kingdom origin of the good being done.

Preaching displays the kingdom as the saving power in the world. In the story of the destruction of Sodom, the Lord agreed with Abraham that he would not destroy it if there could be found ten righteous people in it. So does the kingdom of righteous persons serve as a saving deterrent in our day.

Many other evidences of the kingdom may be displayed by preaching, and many other results of preaching might be listed other than those so briefly touched upon in this chapter. One more may be singled out.

Preaching proves that the preacher is one of the "power people" mentioned in the Preface. By preaching, the preacher has broken through the hard stone face of doubt and evil to lead many into the marvelous light of God.

For our easy remembrance, perhaps the sum of the results of preaching may be encapsulated in the imagining of that gifted preacher, George Buttrick. He thought to himself that every one of his morning congregation came down the aisle before going to the pew and each cast his or her own particular burden on the chancel floor.[5] This is true in a very real sense. People do bring their burdens to church with them. Although we cannot see them lying in a heap before us as we rise to preach, they are there. The people who brought them are wondering if they may leave them there and go from that holy place relieved and rejoicing, or if they must pick them up again and bear them wearily away. If the preaching does what this chapter indicates that it can do, then the hearers will go out to a new day and a new hope and a new start.

However, even if it happens that we are not permitted to know the wide influence of our preaching or that we must preach in a situation that limits the scope of our preaching until we bemoan the fact that little tangible seems to have been achieved, even so, we can whole-heartedly say with Austin Phelps: "To have done *any thing* in such a service [preaching] is a thing to be grateful for for ever."[6]

"If all the tales are told, re-tell them, Brother.
If few attend, let those who listen feel.
Any brave effort will inspire another."[7]

Notes

Introduction

¹Glenn H. Asquith, *Preaching According to Plan* (Valley Forge: Judson Press, 1968), p. 11.

Chapter 1

¹Arthur Hugh Clough, "Say Not the Struggle Nought Availeth," *A Selection from the Great English Poets*, ed. Sherwin Cody (Chicago: A. C. McClurg & Co., 1919), p. 559.
²Reinhold Niebuhr, "Beyond Tragedy," *The Fellowship of the Saints*, ed. Thomas S. Kepler (Nashville: Abingdon Press, 1948), p. 738.
³From *Hyde Park Baptist News*, quoted in *Baptist Leader*.
⁴William Arthur, *The Tongue of Fire* (Old Tappan, N.J.: Fleming H. Revell Co., 1856), pp. 252-253.

Chapter 2

¹Robert Louis Stevenson, "What Is Man?" *The Pursuit of Learning*, ed. Nathan Comfort Starr (New York: Harcourt Brace Jovanovich Inc., 1956), p. 700.
²George A. Buttrick, *Jesus Came Preaching* (New York: Charles Scribner's Sons, 1931), pp. 10-11.
³Lord Cecil, quoted by Ralph Waldo Emerson, *The Complete Writings of Ralph Waldo Emerson*, 2 vols. (Jersey City, N.J.: Wm. H. Wise & Co., 1929), 1:330.
⁴Willard L. Sperry, in *Effective Preaching*, ed. G. Bromley Oxnam (Nashville: Abingdon Press, 1929), p. 71.
⁵Matthew Arnold, "East London," *Masterpieces of Religious Verse*, ed. James Dalton Morrison (New York: Harper & Row, Publishers, Inc., 1948), pp. 499-500.
⁶P. T. Forsyth, *Positive Preaching and Modern Mind* (New York: A. C. Armstrong & Son, 1907), p. 82.

Chapter 3

[1] Tarbell's *Teachers' Guide* (Old Tappan, N.J.: Fleming H. Revell Co., 1943), p. 7.

[2] Douglas C. Macintosh, "What God Is," *My Idea of God*, ed. Joseph Fort Newton (Boston: Little, Brown, & Co., 1926), p. 141.

[3] William James, *The Varieties of Religious Experience*, ed. Joseph Ratner (Secaucus, N.J.: University Books, Inc., 1963), p. 502.

[4] G. K. Chesterton, "The Everlasting Man," *The Pursuit of Learning*, ed. Nathan Comfort Starr (New York: Harcourt Brace Jovanovich Inc., 1956), p. 617.

[5] Blaise Pascal, *Thoughts*, trans. W. F. Trotter (New York: P. F. Collier & Son, 1910), pp. 138-139.

[6] As quoted in Harold Cooke Phillips, *Bearing Witness to the Truth* (Nashville: Abingdon Press, 1949), p. 108.

[7] Jeremy Taylor, "The Vanity and Shortness of Man's Life," *The Fellowship of the Saints*, ed. Thomas S. Kepler (Nashville: Abingdon Press, 1948), p. 359.

[8] Pascal, as quoted in "The Meaning of Manhood," Henry Van Dyke, *The World's Great Sermons*, 10 vols., comp. Grenville Kleiser (New York: Funk & Wagnalls Inc., 1908), 9:241.

[9] Taylor, "The Vanity and Shortness of Man's Life," p. 358.

[10] Hans Küng, *The Christian Challenge* (New York: Doubleday & Co., Inc., 1979), p.172.

[11] Thomas Carlyle, *Sartor Resartus* (New York: Harper & Row, Publishers, Inc., Thomas Y. Crowell, 1893), p. 203.

Chapter 4

[1] Frederic W. H. Myers, *Saint Paul* (London: Macmillan and Co., Ltd., 1923), p. 4.

[2] Ralph Waldo Emerson, "Reality in Preaching," *Effective Preaching*, ed. G. Bromley Oxnam (Nashville: Abingdon Press, 1929), pp. 28-29.

[3] Austin Phelps, *Men and Books* (New York: Charles Scribner's Sons, 1882), p. 31.

[4] W. H. Auden, "Get There If You Can and See the Land You Once Were Proud to Own," *A New Anthology of Modern Poetry*, ed. Seldon Rodman (New York: Literary Guild of America, 1938), p. 377, as quoted in *The English Auden*, by W. H. Auden, edited by Edward Mendelson and published by Random House, Inc., 1978.

[5] "The Telephone Directory," from *Chimney Smoke* by Christopher Morley. J. B. Lippincott; copyright 1919 by Harper & Row, Publishers. Renewed 1947 by Christopher Morley and by permission of Harper & Row.

Chapter 5

[1] As quoted by Arthur John Gossip, *Experience Worketh Hope* (New York: Charles Scribner's Sons, 1945), p. 109.

[2] Sidney Lanier, "Clover," *Poems of Sidney Lanier*, edited by his wife (New York: Charles Scribner's Sons, 1912), p. 22.

[3] *Ibid.*

[4] F. W. Boreham, *Shadows on the Wall* (Nashville: Abingdon Press, 1922), p. 13.

[5] William Shakespeare, *King Richard II*, Act 2, Sc. 1, lines 271-272.